The Birdkee...

Lories and L...

Rebecca K. O'Connor

Lories and Lorikeets

Project Team
Editor: Thomas Mazorlig
Copy Editor: Joann Woy
Indexer: Elizabeth Walker
Series Design: Mary Ann Kahn
Design: Patricia Escabi

TFH Publications
President/CEO: Glen S. Axelrod
Executive Vice President: Mark E. Johnson
Publisher: Christopher T. Reggio
Production Manager: Kathy Bontz

TFH Publications, Inc.
One TFH Plaza
Third and Union Avenues
Neptune City, NJ 07753

Printed and bound in China
11 12 13 14 15   1 3 5 7 9 8 6 4 2

Library of Congress Cataloging-in-Publication Data
O'Connor, Rebecca.
  Lories and lorikeets / Rebecca K. O'Connor.
     p. cm.
  Includes index.
  ISBN 978-0-7938-1482-4 (alk. paper)
  1. Lories. I. Title.
  SF473.L57O36 2011
  636.6'865--dc22

                         2010036225

The Leader in Responsible Animal Care for Over 50 Years!®
www.tfh.com

Contents

Chapter 1
Lory Basics...5

Chapter 2
What Every Lory Needs.........................20

Chapter 3
Lory Feeding and Nutrition 36

Chapter 4
Life WIth Lories 48

Chapter 5
The Healthy Lory...................................62

Chapter 6
Lory Behavior and Training 76

Chapter 7
The Wide World of Lories.....................92

Resources...106

Index 109

1

Lory
Basics

Lories and lorikeets are brightly colored parrots with personalities to match. Many bird lovers have been introduced to lories in zoo aviaries, where you may feed the birds and closely interact with them. Holding up cups of nectar, a visitor quickly finds him- or herself swarmed by a lively and colorful crowd of characters, lapping up their favorite food with strange brushy tongues. I cared for a flock of lories in a walk-though aviary for some time and could never decide which I loved more: watching the clowning lories or the expressions on the faces of their human feeding stands. It is almost impossible not to be smitten by this feathered riot.

Introduction

Spending some time in Australia soon had me captivated by lories, most especially the two species I saw in the wild, the rainbow lorikeets and the scaly-breasted lories. Rainbows, true to their names, have a brilliant array of colors in their feathers and yet somehow manage to disappear into the eucalyptus forests. If you listen though, they are impossible to miss.

They seem to tumble through the trees–hanging upside-down to forage, playing with their flock mates, and making it sound as if no one could possibly throw a party like a lorikeet flock.

I am not alone in my fascination. Lories have captivated thousands of bird enthusiasts, even though many

Lories are acrobatic birds and often hang in odd positions to feed or groom, like this violet-necked lory is doing.

Many zoos have walk-in aviaries housing mixed flocks of lories. Here, rainbow lories and a blue-streaked lory visit a feeding station.

species have not been in aviculture for long. In the 1970s, aviculturists were introduced to many new varieties of lories from New Guinea, and the popularity of these birds increased dramatically. Although the variety of commercially available lory species greatly increased, many countries, including the United States, passed legislation that regulated and limited the importation of wildlife. Wild birds were soon very difficult to procure, and unfortunately, there was still much to learn about the natural history and needs of lories and lorikeets. This was especially true of their nutrition: many aviculturists fed their lories

diets similar to those of other parrots, primarily seed. This lack of proper nutrition shortened life spans and made breeding problematic, and the numbers of some species in captivity dwindled rather than increased.

Today, some species of lories are common in aviculture, while others remain rare or nonexistent. Aviculturists working with the rare species are very dedicated to the survival of captive-bred populations and to a greater understanding of their dietary, physical, and psychological needs. A few of the species mentioned in Chapter 7 are better left in breeding situations and zoological institutions

Lories' beaks and tongues are specialized for feeding primarily on nectar, pollen, and flowers.

the family Psittacidae (containing all the parrots) and of the subfamily Loriinae (containing just the lories and lorikeets). They are often called "brush-tongued" parrots. The exact number of species depends on who you talk to, but at least 50 species of lory and lorikeet are recognized, along with hundreds of subspecies.

So, how do you tell the difference between a lory and a lorikeet? You can think of it much like the difference between a parrot and a parakeet. Lorikeets tend to be smaller and have longer tails, whereas a lory is a larger bird with a shorter tail. However, the names are often synonymous. In Australia, aviculturists tend to refer to all species as lorikeets, whereas in the United States, you may hear all species referred to as lories by some. For the purposes of this book, unless a particular species of lorikeet is mentioned, all of the Loriinae will be referred to as "lories" or "parrots" just to keep it simple.

because of their rarity, but whether common or rare, all species are worth learning about because of their uniqueness and beauty.

Lory or Lorikeet?

The lory and the lorikeet are parrots found in the islands of the tropical South Pacific; they are members of

Physical Characteristics

Lories–with the exception of only a couple of species–are vibrantly colored parrots. They are found in a stunning range of color combinations including green, blue, red, yellow, and even the unusual shade of black. They come in a variety of sizes, ranging from the diminutive 5-inch (13-cm) Wilhemina's lorikeet to the yellow-streaked lory, which is 12 inches (30 cm) long and the size of an Amazon parrot. For the most part, they share many similar characteristics with all other parrots, but lories have a few distinct attributes that are adaptations to their unique diet.

Tongue

Of course, one of the defining characteristics of a lory is its brush tongue, an amazing adaption that allows members of this family of parrots to make nectar and pollen their primary sustenance. The length of the tongue varies, depending on the types of flowers the species has evolved to utilize for food. Some flowers require a longer tongue, giving some lories a tongue so long that they can lick their own eyes!

The proper name for the brushes on the lories' tongue is *papillae*. These papillae are elongated on the tip of the tongue, giving the end a brush-like appearance. The lory loads up its papillae with pollen or nectar and then withdraws its tongue back into its mouth. The papillae are then scraped across a fold of skin in the mouth, removing the food and allowing the lory to swallow it. The length of these papillae vary from species to species, but the longer these papillae are, the more adept the lory is at collecting pollen and nectar and the more likely that it depends on blossoms as a food source.

These papillae are also used to by the bird to drink water. Other parrots scoop up water in their lower mandible, but the lory dips its tongue into water so that the papillae can collect it; then the lory withdraws its tongue and swallows. This is an important feature in a bird as arboreal as the lory, because it allows him to gather dew or raindrops from leaves in the tree canopy rather than spend time on the ground searching for water.

Bands

Breeders place a band on a parrot's leg when the chick is very small and his foot can fit through the hole in the band. When the parrot gets a little bigger and his foot grows, the band can no longer be slipped off. Banding proves that the lory was bred in captivity and not illegally taken from the wild as an adult. It is very likely that the bird you purchase will have a band, but you do not have to leave it on. Active lories can get their bands caught on things and potentially injure themselves. If you want the band removed, ask your veterinarian to cut it off for you. Do not do it yourself.

Beak

Lories have beaks that are very similar to those of other parrots. However, their upper mandible is more elongated than in other parrots of similar size. These beaks are not designed for cracking and shelling seeds and nuts, as they are in other parrots. In fact, lories are not able to digest hard, dry seeds well enough to get all the nutrition they need from nuts and grains. They do eat some soft, half-ripe seeds, shucking these just as other parrots do. When eating fruit, the lory uses its beak to bite chunks out of the fruit's flesh; then, rather than swallowing the fruit whole, it is manipulated within the beak using the tongue. The fruit is pressed against the bird's palate, squeezing out the juice, which is then swallowed. The remaining fruit skin and pip is discarded with a shake of the head.

Feet and Legs

Lories spend most of their time in trees and, whether they are foraging or playing with flock mates, much of this time is spent upside-down. Drinking dew and raindrops off of leaves and gathering pollen or nectar from hanging flowers requires some acrobatics. Thus, lories have very strong feet and legs, along with sharp nails for keeping themselves securely anchored while hanging. Even in a captive environment, lories will frequently hang from the side of their cage in order to eat rather than sit upright on a perch.

Temperament and Behavior

Every bird is a unique individual, but in general, lories are big in the personality department. Few things are more entertaining to a bird lover than watching the antics of an aviary full of lories. Lories enjoy playing and are often hanging, clambering about, and tussling with their flock mates. It is not

Is a Lory Right for You?

Lories are different from other parrots, in that they require a special diet and more effort in their daily care than do most other birds. As a lory owner, you'll need to prepare special foods and spend considerable time cleaning your bird's living area daily to keep him healthy—and you'll have to be prepared to do this work for the rest of your lory's life. Because of their huge personalities, lories can be intimidating to someone who has never owned a parrot. So, before you buy a lory, ask yourself if you are willing to invest the time and if you are truly ready for the responsibility.

Energetic, playful, and social birds, lories often wrestle with their flock mates.

unusual to see them wrestling with one another. They are high-energy birds.

Their boisterous personality makes them responsive to taming and training, but it can also make them challenging birds with which to work. Many lories approach life fearlessly, which is not always to their benefit. A mixed-species aviary can cause problems with aggression in some species and individuals. As pets, many lories are brazen enough to walk or fly right up to the household dog or cat without any fear of consequences. Obviously, if not properly monitored, lories can get into serious danger.

A high-energy lory can also be intimidating to a first-time parrot owner. Someone who is not comfortable with parrots may find herself extremely nervous with a bird so willing to interact. Lories can also be excitable birds, and this excitement can quickly turn into aggression. A bite from a lory can be pretty painful.

Will My Lory Talk?

Some lory species are more likely than others to imitate human language. However, every lory is an individual. Even if, as a species, they are capable of talking, some lories may never say a word. So, buying a lory because you want him to talk is not a good reason. Get a lory because you love his personality and if he talks, consider that a bonus!

Male or Female

In most species of lory, it is impossible to visually tell the difference between a male and a female. The lory breeder may be able to give you a good guess, or she may sex her birds through DNA testing before she sells them. Even if you do not know whether your bird is male or female, unless you plan to breed, gender does not really matter. It is a good idea to know if your bird is female so you can pay attention to any egg-laying problems she may have, but for the most part, sex does not make a difference in lory personality or playfulness.

Their eating habits also makes husbandry a challenge. Because their diet is primarily liquid, their droppings are extremely wet and are projected much farther than are the droppings of other types of parrots. Cleaning up after an indoor lory can be a real chore, and mixing nectar and feeding fresh fruit every day is also time consuming. Without a doubt, lories are not a good pet for everyone. However, if you're already smitten with lories, and you are up to a long-term commitment to daily work, you may feel their charm is absolutely worth the effort.

Finding a Lory

First of all, do not rush into purchasing a lory. They are as challenging as they are rewarding, so be certain of what you are getting into. Talk to some lory breeders and owners. Find out what they love and dislike about keeping their parrots. Investigate all of the different species and see which one is best suited to your living arrangements. A smaller species may make less of a mess than a larger one. If you have close neighbors, consider that some lories have louder voices than others, and some species may tend to have a more subdued personality than their more boisterous cousins. Take your time and consider all the factors involved. Never buy a lory on impulse!

Although you can occasionally find lories in pet stores, if you are a first-time lory buyer, it is a very good idea to find a reputable breeder from whom to purchase your bird or birds. Lories are not simple birds to manage and having the expertise of an experienced lory breeder to lean on can make your life a whole lot less stressful. If you are thinking that you may want to breed lories yourself someday, then you will definitely want a mentor as well.

If you do go to a breeder, ask for references and see if you can view the breeder's facilities. Lories are very messy, so make allowances for fruit debris and the liquid consistency of their droppings; nevertheless, the aviaries should be tidy and clean smelling, and the lories should look healthy. Avoid breeders with overcrowded cages.

It is uncommon to find lories at bird rescues and animal shelters, but it certainly doesn't hurt to check. You could find the perfect bird waiting for you to give him a good second home.

Choosing a Lory

Lories and parrots in general are very good at hiding any illnesses that they have, so be sure that some sort of health guarantee comes with the bird you purchase. That being said, there are a few things that you can look for in judging the overall health of a bird.

Start by viewing the birds from a distance. If you immediately walk right up to the cage, the birds may become stressed from your unfamiliar presence and show signs that you may misinterpret as illness. So, watching from a distance, make sure the birds seem to be getting around well and are bright and alert. If they are comfortable with people, a healthy lory may sit still, with one foot tucked up, but pay close attention to any bird who seems excessively indifferent to your presence or lethargic.

As you approach closer, note those birds who completely

ignore you and sit on their perches with feathers fluffed, especially if they seem to be breathing irregularly or are having trouble balancing on the perch. A healthy bird should be alert to your presence and agile.

Make sure the feathers around the lory's face and nostrils are clean. Discharge from the nostrils can indicate illness. Sometimes these feathers can get a little matted around their beaks from nectar drinking, but make sure the bird has not been vomiting. The feathers beneath the tail, where the vent is located, should also be clean. Matted feathers beneath the tail may indicate some sort of intestinal disorder. The eyes should be bright and clear, and there should be no swelling around them.

If you handle the bird, be sure to feel his breast. You may need the breeder to hold the bird to avoid getting bit, but feeling around the keel bone at the

The cardinal lory is one of the *Chalcopsitta* lories (*C. cardinalis*). This species is very rare in aviculture but fairly abundant in nature.

Hand-Raised Lories

If you want a lory who will be your best friend, you may want to buy one who is hand-raised. This means that the breeder, instead of the parents, has hand-fed the chick part of the time. A lory who is handfed is socialized to humans. Someone who is adept at hand-raising will probably introduce the parrot to a variety of toys, food, and situations, thus making for a very well-adjusted young bird.

center of the breast is a good indicator of a parrot's health. The flesh should be plump. If the keel feels deeply pointed, then the bird is too thin and may have underlying health issues.

Remember that, even after you purchase a healthy-looking bird, it's still a good idea to have an experienced avian veterinarian exam him.

Types of Lories

Although all species of lory have very similar habits and needs, they come from several different genera and therefore can physically look very different. All share the traits of their brush tongue and similar eating habits, but they come from different places and have different body shapes and different colors. Scientists divide these differences among the Loriinae subfamily of parrots into genera (singular: genus) and species. Some of the genera tend to be more aggressive, some tend to be louder, and some are arguably more suitable as pets than others.

Chalcopsitta

Lories from the genus *Chalcopsitta*, called glossy lories, are large and stout compared to other Loriinae. They all have an area of naked skin around the lower mandible and eye. This is not very obvious because of the skin's black coloration, which is the same as the beak. Birds in this genus tend to have normal vocalizations that are harsh and very loud. They also tend to be aggressive toward other species of birds. A well-known species of this

Children and Lories

Should you get a lory for your child? Probably not. Lories require more work than many other pet birds, and it is likely that adults in the house will soon be caring for the bird. If the child is very young, an excitable lory can be very intimidating as well. However, if you have your heart set on a lory, and you want to let your child help with age-appropriate chores, then that's a great idea. Just make sure that she understands how to interact with your lory appropriately and respectfully.

genus is the black lory (*C. atra*), which is uncommon in the United States.

Charmosyna

Lories in the genus *Charmosyna* are often called ornamental or honey lories, and this is the largest genus of lories. These are small- to medium-sized lories with pointed tails. Their tails may be longer or shorter than their wings, depending on the species. These lories come in a variety of colors, with prominent coloration including red, green, yellow, and blue. All species have a red beak.

The *Charmosyna* have longer tongues than do other lories and feed more with their tongues than do some other species. This makes them slightly more specialized feeders, requiring more liquid in their diets. These species are somewhat sexually dimorphic, meaning that males and females look different. A fairly well known species from this genus is the Stella's lorikeet (*C. papou stellae*), a subspecies of the Papuan lorikeet. Most species of *Charmosyna* are rare or nonexistent in aviculture.

Eos

Lories in the genus *Eos* are referred to as the red lories because of their predominately red coloration, although most species are also marked with blue,

The blue-streaked lory is one of the most popular of the *Eos* lories. They are originally from the Tanimbar Islands of Indonesia.

Breeders in the United States have had success with yellow-bibbed lories (*Lorius chlorocercus*) but they are still rare in aviculture and not available as pets.

purple, and black. They are between 9 and 12 inches (23 and 30 cm) in length, with short, broad tails and beaks that are either orange-red or yellow-orange. Species belonging to the genus *Eos* exude a musky odor. Some members of the species, such as the blue-streaked

lory (*E. reticulata*), are common in aviculture.

Glossopsitta

Members of the genus *Glossopsitta* are very small lories ranging 6 to 9 inches (15 to 22 cm). They have wedge-shaped tails and a black, red-and-black, or orange beak. These species are all native to Australia, and are all very rare in aviculture outside of Australia. In Australia, the purple-crowned lorikeet (*G. porphyrocephala*) and musk lorikeet (*G. concinna*) are widely kept in aviculture.

Lorius

Members of the genus *Lorius* are sometimes called broad-tailed lories, and this genus contains medium-sized, stocky birds with rounded tails and slightly broader and less pointed beaks, thus making them more closely resemble seed-eating parrots. Their beaks are coral red in color. All species also have green wings, in sharp contrast to their red bodies. Most species also have some purple coloration accenting the red. Their size ranges from 10.2 to 16 inches (26 to 41 cm). Their normal vocalizations, although not as loud as some parrots, do carry a long way and can be a concern to neighbors. They also tend to be aggressive to other parrot-like birds. Some species, such as the chattering lory (*L. garrulus garrulus*), are common and much sought after in aviculture.

Neopsittacus

The genus *Neopsittacus*, sometimes called mountain lories, contains two species from the mountains of New Guinea. Both are small lories with long tails. They are similar to *Charmosyna* and *Oreopsittacus* but have a bill that is broader and more heavily built than species from these other genera. This broad bill and a more developed gizzard allow this genus to consume more seed than do other lories. The Musschenbroek's or yellow-billed lorikeet (*N. musschenbroekii*) can be found in aviculture, but is not common.

Oreopsittacus

There is only one species of lory in the genus *Oreopsittacus*, and it is not a common one in aviculture. The whiskered or plum-faced lorikeet (*O. arfaki*) is a small lory, only 6 inches (15 cm) long. It is native to New Guinea, where it resides at high altitudes (8,000 to 12,000 feet [2,400 to 3,700 m]). The whiskered lorikeet is primarily a green parrot, and the male and the female can be differentiated by their coloration. Males have a brightly colored forehead and face of red and mauve. This species is unique not only to lories, but to all parrots because it has 14 tail feathers instead of the universal standard of 12 feathers.

Phigys

The genus *Phigys* also has only one species. Many taxonomists, however, believe that that this species is not distinct enough from the genus *Vini* to warrant a separate genus. A brightly

The collared lory of Fiji is the only member of the genus *Phigys*. In their native islands, these birds have adapted fairly well to urban areas.

colored, primarily red lory with accents of green and deep purple, the collared lory (*P. solitarus*) is unusual in aviculture, although the San Diego Zoo has had some success in breeding them. They are found in the Fiji Islands in the wild and are a fairly small bird at 8 inches (20 cm) long.

Pseudeos

Pseudeos is a genus of only one species as well, the dusky lory (*P. fuscata*), which is prolific in the wild and very common in aviculture. They are native to New Guinea. The dusky lory is about 10 inches (25 cm) long and comes in two color phases—orange or yellow—with accents of dark brown feathering. All have bright orange eyes and beaks. They are one of the easiest lories to find in aviculture, as experienced aviculturalists have had great success in breeding them.

Trichoglossus

The *Trichoglossus* genus encompasses some of the most common and sought-after lories in aviculture. This is a broad genus, with species that appear very different from one another and birds that range geographically from Indonesia, New Guinea, coastal Australia, and even the Carolina Islands. Some species are common in the wild, whereas others are geographically isolated and not well known. They range in size from 6 inches (16 cm) to 12 inches (30 cm). One of the most well-known species is the rainbow lorikeet (*T. haematodus*).

Vini

Birds of the genus *Vini* are sometimes referred to as virgin or fringe parrots. They are all lories from small island populations. All of these species are having a very difficult time in the wild due to introduced rats and habitat

Unweaned Parrots

Some people suggest that parrots have the best relationship with the person who hand-raises them and that potential owners should purchase unweaned parrots. This is simply not true. A lory who is well socialized during hand-raising is just as wonderful whether you bring him home before he is weaned or feeding himself. Hand-feeding lories can be challenging and dangerous for the parrot if done by someone inexperienced. In fact, it is illegal to sell unweaned parrots in some states. You are much better off buying a weaned parrot.

The rainbow lorikeet is the most common species in captivity. In nature, it is found from Indonesia and New Guinea south to Tasmania and east to New Caledonia and Vanuatu.

destruction. In fact, two species are known to be extinct. The remaining five species are colorful, stout, and small lories only 7.5 to 8 inches (19 to 20 cm) long. None are readily available in the pet market. The Rimatara or Kuhl's lorikeet (*V. kuhlii*) is a brightly colored green, yellow, and red bird with deep purple accents that has been recently part of a successful reintroduction program in the Cook Islands.

The subfamily of Loriinae are a fascinating and colorful group, with many species endangered in the wild and unusual in aviculture. Understanding this, it is important to learn all you can about your lory before you bring him home or, if you already have a lory, to expand your knowledge so that you can provide the best possible environment for your bird. You will need more than just some fruit and a cage for your new friend—you will need to make sure that your lory has everything he needs to play, explore, sleep, and—above all—remain happy and healthy.

2

What Every Lory Needs

Like all birds, a lory who lives in your home needs an environment that simulates his experiences in the wild as closely as possible. Of course, your home will be nothing like the jungle, but you should do the best you can to provide your lory with as much room as possible, with a safe and clean living area, and with plenty of toys and experiences to occupy his mind. The most important piece of equipment is his cage.

Cages

Before you bring your lory home, the first thing you must have in place is an appropriate cage. So many different styles of parrot cages are available that choosing the right one can be confusing. Also, a cage that is appropriate for a parrot similar to the size of your lory may not be quite right for your bird. So, what do you need? First, you need to decide if you are keeping your lory indoors or outdoors. If you are just starting out in the world of lories, it is probably best to provide your bird with an indoor cage and an opportunity to play safely outside of his cage.

Indoor Caging

If you are thinking of getting a single lory, you probably want your new friend to live indoors with you. Lories

Some lory enthusiasts recommend using a rabbit cage or a metal dog crate like this one for housing lories.

Where to Put the Cage

Consider these things when placing your lory's cage:

- **Activity**: Will your lory be where he can interact with everyone?
- **Air movement**: Avoid drafty areas
- **Safety**: Is the cage away from dangers like fireplaces, stovetops, or hazardous chemicals?
- **Sunlight**: Put your lory in a well-lit area, but out of direct sunlight
- **Traffic**: Will people run into the cage or startle your lory?

have a reputation for being rather messy because of their diet and the liquid state of their droppings. However, the mess isn't greater than that of other pet birds, just different. So, there's no reason why you can't set up your lory inside.

Cage Placement

Give some thought to setting up the cage so that dealing with clean-up is not too much of a problem. Choose an area that gets a lot of light (but not direct sunlight, which can cause your lory to overheat), that is free from chilling drafts, and that is easy to clean. You also want to make sure that your lory will be in the middle of family activities, but not someplace where he will be constantly startled or have his cage knocked into frequently.

Cage Size

Where you place the cage may dictate to some degree how big a cage your lory can have. The rule of thumb with any parrot, of course, is the bigger

the better. Lories come in a variety of sizes, and smaller lories may do fine in a cockatiel-sized cage. The larger species may need something more in the size range of what an Amazon parrot would like. It's most important that your lory can turn, flap his wings, hop, and play without being too restricted inside his cage. You'll also want to be absolutely certain that the cage's bar spacing is appropriate. Bars should be close enough together so that your lory cannot slip his head through and accidentally hang himself.

Other Considerations

Despite its size, a standard parrot cage may not be the best solution for a lory's living arrangements. Lories are more active than most parrots, seemingly nonstop in their play. Because they are constantly hanging from the sides and top of their cages, hopping, and climbing, they require larger caging than most parrot species of comparable sizes. How a lory plays also means

Lories do well in outdoor aviaries, provided you take some precautions against predators and inclement weather. This is a dusky lory.

a cage rather than a plastic carrier–also make great homes for lories. Just make sure that the bar spacing is right and that the wire is not galvanized–galvanized wire contains zinc, and zinc can be toxic to nibbling parrots.

Remember that your lory's cage will require frequent, thorough cleaning. A lory will get his living quarters sticky and filthy quicker than will a regular parrot, thus allowing bacteria and mold to grow if it's not cleaned regularly. Light cages will be easier to carry outside to be hosed down. If you are considering a large wrought-iron cage, be sure it has wheels and will be easy to roll outside to be hosed and scrubbed.

Consider a cage with a removable grate and a deep bottom. A cage with a deep bottom will catch more debris, and the grate will keep your lory from getting down into the mess. If the grate is easily removed, you can scrub it as needed. Also consider ease of access to bowls and food holders from outside the cage.

that a cage that is wider than it is tall is a better fit for an active lory than is standard tall but narrow parrot caging. Many lory owners have had great success using rabbit or ferret cages for their birds. Others have found that wire dog kennels–the kind that resemble

Outdoor Caging

If you are contemplating setting up an aviary for multiple lories, you may want to consider outdoor caging. Keep in mind, however, that many lories do not do well in mixed-species groups or with multiple pairs. Look into species tendencies before you decide to set up more than two birds. If you do set up outdoor caging, two styles are common: a traditional aviary or a suspended aviary. Both should provide birds with shelter from wind and rain, while simultaneously providing excellent ventilation.

Whichever one you choose to build, consider your area's climate.

You must make sure that your lories do not get too hot in the summer or too cold in the winter. Some species are more tolerant of heat and cold than others, so research to make sure that your lories will be comfortable and safe.

Walk-In Aviaries

Traditional walk-in aviaries are preferred by those who want an outdoor enclosure that complements their garden or backyard. Some people have had luck with nontoxic, bird-safe plantings inside a traditional aviary, but for the most part, lories do an excellent job of destroying live plants. If you

This walk-in aviary has two highly recommended features: a safety porch and a concrete floor.

Keeping It Tropical

Concerned that your home might be too hot or too cold for your lory? Don't worry. If you can stand the heat or cold, so can your lory. The exception to this is leaving him in a direct draft, where he might become chilled, or in direct sunlight, where he might overheat. You may need to set the thermostat to a reasonable range if you leave for the day or evening in extreme weather, but for the most part, if you can take it, your lory can too.

don't mind replacing the vegetation, however, busy lories are happy lories!

In a walk-in aviary, concrete flooring with good drainage is preferable to dirt floors. Dirt floors are difficult to keep sanitary and can harbor fungus, mold, and bacteria. All aviaries require constant cleaning, so any design should take this into consideration. In a traditional aviary, you will also want to include a safety porch so that an enclosed room stands between your birds and the outside world before you step inside with them. Fully enclosed sleeping quarters can also keep birds safe and warm during the winter.

Suspended Aviaries

Many lory enthusiasts prefer suspended caging. These cages are generally rectangular and made entirely of welded wire, without a solid floor. They can be suspended from the ceiling or set up on a base with legs, with the bottom of the cage 4 feet (1.5 m) or so above a concrete floor, so that excess food, debris, and droppings fall through the bottom and sides of the cage and away from the birds. The concrete floor can then be hosed and scrubbed daily. The wire mesh sides and bottom of a suspended cage will also need to be scrubbed frequently, but cleaning will be easier than with a traditional fully floored enclosure.

Suspended cages work well for breeding lories kept in single pairs. Often lory breeders who keep their birds in this type of caging will put all their lories together in a large aviary after the breeding season has ended, giving the birds a larger space to fly around in.

Sleeping Cages

If your lory will live indoors, many parrot owners recommend a sleeping cage. Although no studies have been done on the subject, many parrot enthusiasts believe that parrots need 10 to 12 hours of sleep at night. They also argue that a parrot who does not get enough sleep can develop behavioral problems. If your lory lives in the middle of the daily hubbub, such as in the living room of a household where activity starts before dawn and ends well after dark, consider giving him another place in which to sleep at night.

A sleeping cage can be much smaller than a daytime cage, and it does not need to be loaded with toys. Place it in a room where the bird will not be disturbed; the idea is to give your bird a quiet place to settle in for the night. Whether or not your bird needs the sleep, if he is active and noisy, a sleeping cage for your lory may be a great idea for you, so that you can wind down for your last few hours of the night and not be woken before dawn. Just remember that a sleeping cage is not meant to give you

an excuse to ignore your busy lory, but to give everyone a reasonable amount of time to relax and sleep.

Play Areas

Even if you've bought your lory the biggest cage possible, it is still a cage. Your lory should also have an area where he can get out and play. Many cages come with play tops, and this may be the most convenient option. Another possibility is a movable play stand complete with branches, bowls, and toys, as well as a large base to catch droppings or debris.

Many lory lovers find that a queen-sized sheet on the floor, supplied with lory toys for play and investigation, also makes a great play area. When

Like other parrots, your indoor lory needs to have play areas outside of his cage. This is a Goldie's lorikeet on a wooden play stand.

Does My Lory Need a Nestbox?

Some lory experts recommend giving lories a nestbox to sleep in—even if they are single birds—because many lories seem to prefer to sleep in a nest at night whether or not they are sitting on eggs. If your lory is a single female, however, it might not be a good idea to give her a nestbox. Having a nest could stimulate egg laying, which can make her territorial and aggressive, and may increase the chance that she could become egg bound.

play time is over, the sheet can easily be folded up and stored or thrown into the washing machine if it's time to clean it.

Keeping it all Clean

Although lories get a bad rap for the liquid consistency of their droppings, they are easy to manage. Whether or not you consider lories the messiest of all parrot species definitely depends on your definition of "messy." The nice thing about lories is that you do not have to clean up seed husks and shells. You also do not have to worry so much about their destructive beaks. Lory beaks are not designed to crack hard nuts and shells, and they are not likely to do much damage to your furniture. However, you do have to deal with a liquid and definitely sticky mess.

One of the most effective means of keeping your lory area clean is to hang acrylic panels on three sides of your bird's cage. These panels can then be removed and scrubbed as needed. Shower curtains will also work, but are likely to be chewed and will not last as long. You can also purchase acrylic cages, but then your lory does not have cage bars on which to hang and monkey around. Hanging acrylic panels gives you and your bird the best of both worlds. Most lory owners also buy plastic floor mats, like those used beneath office chairs, to place under cages to protect carpet or wood flooring.

You can also use sheets around the bottom of the cage to catch sticky droppings and liquid food—your bird won't produce so much mess that a sheet can't catch it all. If you do not want to hang panels from the sides of the cage, try hanging plastic sheeting on the wall behind it. Plastic sheeting, such as that used when painting, is inexpensive and can be torn down and replaced as needed.

Keep in mind as well that the closer your lory's cage is to the floor, the less distance any mess will travel from the cage—this is another reason why a tall rather than a wide cage is not necessarily an ideal choice. If you have other animals that might bother the lory in your house, having the cage close to the floor may not be an option, however.

All of these precautions should help

keep the area surrounding your lory in good shape, but you will also need to clean your lory's cage frequently. A quick daily cleaning is necessary, and then, every week or so, a thorough cleaning and disinfecting is in order.

Daily cleaning should involve scrubbing all food, water, and bathing bowls. You should also clean out the bottom of your lory's cage every day. The best substrate to catch debris and droppings is newspaper, which is nontoxic and is easy to gather up, throw away, and replace. Then, a quick wipe down will keep your bird's cage from getting overly sticky.

Once a week, move your parrot to a safe place and take his cage outside for a good hosing down and scrubbing. Hosing the cage and letting it sit for a bit will allow the spattered nectar, fruit, and droppings to soften up, making it easier to scrub off caked-on debris with a fiber brush. Once all the debris is scrubbed off, disinfect the cage with a solution of bleach and water (about one part bleach to nine parts water). Allow the cage to sit in the sun for a while, then rinse it thoroughly. If you can't take the cage outside, wash, bleach,

and leave it in the bathtub to disinfect (if it will fit). If neither option works for your situation, you can clean the cage in place. Be careful so you don't get bleach on anything that it will discolor or damage.

Don't forget to scrub and disinfect perches as well. It may be easiest to remove all perches and toys, and scrub and disinfect them in the sink. Most plastic or metal items can be put in the dishwasher (in a load separate from your family's dishes and utensils), which is probably the easiest and most effective way to get everything clean. Keeping your lory's cage, toys, and

Because they primarily feed on nectar and fruit, lories are a bit messier than most other parrots. This is a scaly-breasted lory.

play area clean and disinfected can go a long way toward keeping your pet healthy.

Pest Controls

If you live in a temperate climate, you may find that keeping things clean is critical to keeping pest problems under control. Ants and cockroaches may be especially interested in the sugary area surrounding your lory's cage. If you find you are having difficulty keeping pests out of your bird's area, go cautiously with chemical controls. Most pesticides are toxic to birds, so keeping things scrupulously clean may be your best—and safest—defense. Standing the legs of the cage in shallow bowls of water makes it difficult for insects to cross and climb into the cage, and this may be enough to keep your lory safe from some crawling insects.

Living Accessories

In addition to caging and play areas, your lory needs other small accessories for comfortable day-to-day living. Most are not terribly expensive, but do require consideration and thought.

Perching

Lories are busy birds, and perching is an important aspect of their housing. You should have as much strategically placed perching available as possible without making their living space too cluttered. Try to supply a variety of sizes, diameters, and textures as well, which is healthy for a parrot's feet. Avoid perches that are slick and difficult for the lory to grasp. Natural

Natural wooden branches make excellent perches. Their varying diameter and texture will help keep your lory's feet in top condition.

perches are best. If you have pesticide-free fruit trees in your yard, these make great perches, and they allow your bird to strip leaves and bark, making them a great toy as well as a place to stand. When the perches are worn, they can also easily be replaced. While rope perches are good for other parrots, lories usually turn them into a sticky, nasty mess, so you should avoid them.

Bowls

When you purchase bowls, be sure to choose hard plastic, ceramic, or metal. Your bird's bowls will need frequent washing, so select ones that are easy to clean. Make sure you purchase plenty of extras as well. Because some of the foods you offer will only keep for a few hours, you may be replacing or pulling out bowls to be cleaned frequently. You can save yourself time by having a clean set always available while others are in the dishwasher waiting to be washed.

Bath Pans

Lories love a good bath, and you will want to make sure that your bird has bowls or pans of an appropriate size in which to bathe. Some lories may take several baths a day, especially in warm

Most lories like toys they can manipulate and throw around and also ones that make noise.

weather. Choose heavy, shallow bowls that are difficult to tip over. Make sure the water isn't so deep that your lory can drown—a few inches (cm) of water is plenty for a bath.

Lighting

As you gather all the necessities for your lory, don't forget that sunlight is an important part of good health for most animals. A well lit room is important, but it still may not be enough. Sunlight shining through a window loses ultraviolet rays and much of its health benefits. If your bird does not get time outside, consider

Lories love to play with toys on the bottom of their cages. Your lory may even roll over on his back in his excitement.

purchasing full-spectrum lighting. You can get lights that provide both UVB and UVA (types of ultraviolet light) online, in pet stores, and in hardware stores. Place the lights near, but not directly on the cage.

Environmental Enrichment

One of the most important things that you can provide your busy, intelligent lory is environmental enrichment. This means plenty of things to keep his mind, beak, and feet busy. A lory in the wild is constantly on the go. If your lory does not have enough to do in his cage and in your home, he can develop behavioral problems and in general

will not be as mentally stimulated and healthy as he could be. The good news is that it is not hard to entertain a lory.

Hanging and Foot Toys

Since lories are not chewers, focus on toys that are fun and easy to clean. Lories will play with just about anything. Look for plastic toys that can be scattered on the bottom of the cage and easily manipulated. Whiffle balls can bring hours of entertainment. Lories also seem to gravitate toward toys that make noise. A small bottle with beads inside that clatter and rattle is another toy that a lory will appreciate playing with on the floor of his cage.

Lories also enjoy hanging toys, so festoon his cage with plastic keys, bottle caps, or beads strung on rawhide strips or suspended from a quick link. Soft, chewable wood, like pine, might get some attention but keep in mind that wooden toys are difficult to clean and disinfect. Lories also love a hanging swing. Use your imagination, and you may discover that your lory can have fun with just about anything!

Be sure to consider safety when you give your lory toys. Make sure that there is no way to get a toe, beak, or head stuck in a toy somehow. If you have any cloth or rope in your bird's cage, watch for fraying and strings and remove worn ropes immediately. Birds can get toes and necks wrapped in a loose string, and this can be disastrous.

Edible Toys

Some of the best toys are actually edible. Fruits and vegetables hung from steel kebabs are a great way for a lory to entertain himself. In the wild, lories hang upside down or climb nimbly along branches, tasting fruit and tonguing flowers. Hanging safe flowers such as bottlebrush (*Callistemon* spp.), which wild Australian lories feed on, within his cage will give your lory something to do while he eats. Be inventive: give your parrot a situation that makes him forage and explore in order to get his food. This is much more fun and entertaining for you both than simply having him find his food in a bowl.

Rotating Toys

Old toys are boring toys. The great thing about a bird who prefers plastic indestructible toys is that, over the years, your lory toy collection will grow and grow. So, every few days, trade out the toys in his cage for a new set. If he hasn't seen a particular toy in a few weeks, it will much more interesting than the same old toys he sees every day. Rotate toys in and out of the cage and keep your lory interested in the selection. This will also help you keep his toys as clean as possible.

Safety

As you gather up all the goodies that will keep your lory happy and healthy, don't forget to make your home parrot-safe. A bird as active and fearless as a lory can quickly get himself into trouble. So, be aware of the dangers both inside and outside of the cage.

Foraging

A wonderful way to provide environmental enrichment for your lory is to teach him to forage for food. In the wild, lories spend all day searching for and finding food. You can emulate this by setting up food in various places around the cage and by hiding bits of fruit and vegetables in cereal boxes, brown paper bags, or anything thing else that can be torn up and thrown away. If you teach your lory to look for treats in hidden places around his cage, he will have something to keep him busy for a while.

Inside the Cage

While watching out for worn or dangerous toys, also consider zinc. Zinc is poisonous to parrots and can be ingested through galvanized metals. Zinc toxicity can cause feather plucking, gastric distress, or even death, depending on how much zinc gets into the bird's system.

Also watch out for anything small enough to swallow, remembering that larger toys can be broken into small pieces that can be swallowed and obstruct the throat. Keep an eye on your parrot when you give him a new toy; breaking and eating toys is not as big an issue with lories as with other parrots, but it's better to keep an eye out whenever you offer a new toy to your bird.

Watch out for smoke and other airborne irritants as well. Many things we put in the air are bad for us, and many stories of the dangers are overblown. However, as a rule of thumb, if it smells strongly to you, don't put it or use it near your bird's cage. One exception to this rule is over-heated Teflon, which doesn't smell but rapidly kills birds. When you have a lory, avoid using Teflon-coated pans, irons, space heaters, and other such appliances. And keep in mind that if something is dangerous to your bird, maybe you shouldn't have it in your house in the first place—it probably is not very good for you either.

Be mindful as well of where you get your lory's food and of how long it has been in the cage. Keep your bird's food fresh and free of mold and fungus. Feed fresh food from dependable sources that don't use pesticides. Some crops, like strawberries and raspberries, are more heavily sprayed with pesticides than others, so only buy these items when they are certified organic.

Outside of the Cage

Be sure to lory-proof your home outside of the cage, as well. A lory who is out and about can get into a lot of trouble, especially if he is *flighted* (that is, does not have his wings clipped to

Do You Need a Pair?

People often imagine that their parrots will be lonely without a mate. This is not really true. Your parrot has you to keep him company, and if you get him a mate he may no longer be interested in having a friendship with you. However, parrots living in separate cages in the same room seem to enjoy the flock environment. They may communicate back and forth, and eat, play, and nap at the same time. Of course, this means more noise, more mess, and less time for you to spend with each bird. So, there is a trade-off to consider when you decide if you would rather have one parrot or more.

Placing some of your lory's food on stakes or kebabs so that he has to climb or hang to get it will help keep him busy in his cage or aviary.

prevent flying). A flying bird may be hurt or killed by a ceiling fan, a pot of water boiling on the stove, or an open fireplace. Many a bird has also been injured by flying into windows that look as though they might lead directly to the outside. Make sure than blinds and curtains are closed whenever your lory is outside his cage. Be mindful of standing water in general; birds may drown in dog bowls, toilets, fish tanks, and fountains.

Even a lory who is not flighted can get into trouble. Make sure that your lory cannot encounter any other pets in the household such as dogs, cats, snakes, and ferrets. Even larger parrots may spell trouble for a brazen lory. Also make sure that no poisonous substances are available for a lory to explore. Lories tend to use their tongues to examine things. So poisonous plants, pesticides, lead, cleansers, and all other household toxins should be nowhere within the reach of your bird.

3

Lory Feeding and Nutrition

Nutrition is perhaps the most important thing to consider before you bring home a lory. Lories are the most selective eaters of all parrots, sustaining themselves on a very unique diet in the wild. They have a short digestive tract, which means that food must pass through quickly. They also have a *ventriculus* or gizzard that is less muscular than that of most birds, and therefore they do not have the ability to derive nutrition from the hard, dry seeds that other parrots eat.

Scientists still need to do more research to discover the exact nutritional needs of lories in captivity. So, although captive lory diets are much better than ever before, there is still much to learn. As a lory lover, you must be committed to keeping up with the most recent nutritional science concerning your pet, and you must also be committed to the work involved in preparing fresh food not just once, but several times a day.

Wild Eating

Whichever species of lory you decide is the right one to bring into your home, the very first thing you should do is find out where that species lives

Lories feed heavily on flowers—such as this Australian bottlebrush (*Callistemon* spp.)—in the wild. However, the dietary needs of each species differ, so you have to learn what's best for yours.

in the wild and what it eats. As you may have discovered in Chapter 1, most species of lory are only native to very tiny areas, such as isolated islands. Thus, every species of lory may have a slightly different diet that depends on its native location and what's available during various seasons. In general, lories primarily feed on nectar, pollen, flowers, buds, insects, and even some soft, unripe seeds. However, the percentage of each of these items in the diet differs among the various lory species.

The more specialized the tongue and the longer the papillae, the more dependent a lory species is on nectar in the wild. This doesn't mean that you need to find the exact plants your bird would be eating in the wild, but it does mean that your parrot's diet may benefit from certain additions to his diet. The specifics of this will change as researchers discover more about what lories eat in their native habitats. Fortunately, with the Internet, it is easier than ever to hear about these scientific discoveries. So, pay attention—not to everything that is said on the Internet, but to those scientists and avian veterinarians who are researching the best possible care for your lory.

When Nutrition is Insufficient

For a long time, lory owners simply did not know what was appropriate to feed their birds. This was not because they were negligent; it was because no one understood what brush-tongued parrots needed to survive and thrive in

Supplements

Wondering if you should give your lory supplements? If you are feeding him commercial nectar and plenty of fresh fruits and vegetables, there is really no need. In fact, you can actually make a bird ill by overdosing him on certain vitamins and minerals. Unless your vet prescribes them, avoid the supplements and just give your lory a healthy varied diet.

captivity. Early captive lories were fed seeds and homemade diets based on superstitious guesses that were based more on wishful thinking than science. Because they did not get sufficient nutrition, these lories died of "fits" and "cramps," and had significantly shortened lives. They also rarely bred in captivity.

As lory fanciers worked hard to getting their birds' diets right, the birds began to live longer and breed more successfully. When it comes to lories, more literature is available on diets than on anything else, and almost all of it is anecdotal. Even today, if their nutrition is not quite right, lories may have significant color differences in their plumage and be subject to diseases and shortened lives. Fortunately, we are a lot closer to providing lories with exactly what they need than we were ten years ago. The continuing challenge to discover the optimal diet for every lory species underlines how incredibly important it is for lory owners to not take short cuts and to feed their birds the best, most varied diet possible.

Old Diets

For a long time, no manufactured feeds for lories were available and everyone had to make her own homemade diet. Milk-based baby cereal and tinned milk with the addition of honey or glucose was the basis of many lory formulas. Even as manufactured diets were developed, many breeders continued to stick with whatever homemade formula worked for them. Because no one was quite certain which ingredients in their recipes helped their lories to thrive, they played it safe and stuck to what worked. However, there have been a few shared assumptions.

Based on the understanding that pollen is very high in protein, breeders and successful lory enthusiasts have mostly agreed that lories require a diet high in protein. It was also agreed that lories required a diet high in sugar because of the amount of nectar they consumed. Even some of these assumptions are changing, but for the most part a commercial nectar, given in addition to a variety of fruits and vegetables, should keep your lory healthy and thriving.

Nectar

Nectar is an important component of daily nutrition for lories, and all lories seem to really thrive when they have it in their diets. Lories who are fed nectar are healthier and live longer. So, most lory enthusiasts include some form of nectar in their birds' diets. There are two kinds of nectar. One is water soluble; it comes in a dry form and is mixed with water to create liquid nectar. The other is not water soluble and is fed dry. The dry form is less expensive and keeps longer once placed in the cage, but many people prefer to feed nectar in a liquid form. Some breeders mix their own nectar, but the average lory owner should choose a proven commercial diet, so that you can be sure that the food you offer your pet is safe and completely nutritious.

Be careful when giving lories liquid nectar. In hot environments, nectar spoils quickly, but lories may not stop eating it. During hot summer weather, remove nectar after a few hours so that bacteria cannot contaminate it and

Fresh Food Daily

Lories need fresh food daily, no exception. Other birds may be left for a day with some seeds or pellets and water, but not lories. Everything that lories eat can spoil, and eating spoiled food can make them ill. Put fresh food in with them at least once a day, and twice is preferable.

Whether you feed it liquid or dry (as seen here), nectar should be a component of your lory's diet.

make your bird ill. In cooler weather, you may be able to leave it all day. The best plan is to feed your bird just as much nectar as he will eat within an hour or two, so that nothing is wasted.

Several brands of nectar are available, and some are considered complete diets, but an active bird like a lory should be fed a variety of foods if only for the environmental enrichment it provides him. It's important that your lory have a choice of fresh foods at all times.

Fruits & Vegetables

Lories enjoy browsing a variety of foods, and the larger the variety of foods you offer your lory, the better off he will be. Rather than offering one or two large portions in a feeding, offer small quantities of as many items as possible. This allows your bird to have a greater range of choice in his nutrition and keeps him intrigued and occupied.

All of the fruits and vegetables that are fed to other parrots can be given to lories as well. They should be uncooked to retain the most nutrients possible. Many lories enjoy melons, papaya, mango, kiwi, apple, berries, and any other seasonal fruits. You can also offer carrots, peas, peppers, and dark leafy greens, such as collards and

Don't Feed Sugar

Do not be tempted to make up your own nectar using sugar and water. Sugar is not a good diet for lories. It does not have the complex set of nutrients that lories need to stay healthy. Lories, however, do not know this and think it tastes wonderful. In Australia, it is not unusual to see them raiding sugar packets from outdoor restaurants. Like children, lories will lap up sugar and sugary drinks if are they offered and pass over the nutritious foods they need. Skip the sugar and give your lory a commercial nectar.

mustard greens, to your lory.

Fresh is always a good choice when choosing fruits and vegetables, but frozen is a close second—if not sometimes better. Frozen foods are usually frozen almost immediately after being harvested, which means that they retain more nutrients than does fresh produce that has to travel to the grocery store. Of course, the very best foods are fresh out of your garden. So, if you have room, consider growing food both for your table and for your bird. Canned vegetables should be avoided as they are almost always high in sodium and are not as nutritious. They are also not as flavorful and may not be as readily accepted by your lory.

A great way to offer fruits and vegetables is to finely dice the item into a "chop." This potentially stops a bird from picking out his favorite and possibly less nutritious bits. Some breeders also make a puree by mixing fruits and vegetables into a consistency like applesauce. When you feed a puree, less produce will be flung about

to rot, and you can feed just as much as your bird will eat in an hour or so.

If you chop or puree fruits and vegetables for the sake of nutrition, then you should still offer whole fruits and vegetables of preference for the sake of fun. Occasionally hang large pieces of produce for your lory to both eat and investigate. A busy bird is a happy bird.

Sprouts

It's a great idea to sprout seeds for your lories. Although lories cannot digest hard seeds, they do well with sprouted seeds. Once seeds are soaked, they soften and begin to grow, and once the seeds begin to show short sprouts, they are ready to be fed to your bird. Seeds germinated in this way are very high in nutrition and easy to digest, making them a great addition to your lory's diet.

Be sure to sprout your own. Grocery store sprouts may not be as fresh and therefore not as nutritious. And be careful about the seeds that you buy to sprout as well. Do not buy seeds that are meant for sowing in your garden–these may be treated with chemicals. Instead, choose seeds sold specifically for sprouting; you can find these at health food stores and online. To sprout seeds, simply rinse the seeds, soak them overnight or until sprouts emerge, rinse again, and serve. Sprout small batches at a time to avoid spoilage.

About Pellets

Most parrots now have pellets designed to be fed as their primary diet. Parrot enthusiasts who keep birds other than lories have had a great deal of success with these pelleted diets, especially with the addition of some seed and a generous helping of fruits and vegetables. So, it's not surprising that pellet manufactures would create a pelleted diet for lories. Some lory enthusiasts do feed their birds pellets, but lories prefer these pellets soaked, and they are generally only included as an addition to nectar, fruits, and vegetables.

Some fanciers believe that these pellets make a lory's droppings firmer and therefore less messy. In my opinion, however, convenience is not a good reason to change a bird's diet. If you think your lory would enjoy the variety of some soaked pellets in his diet, however, there is probably no harm in including them as a treat.

New Thoughts on Lory Diets

Research is slowly refining the knowledge base on feeding lories and, in the near future, we may figure out exactly what these beautiful birds need for optimum health. Debra McDonald,

Lories enjoy most fruits. Offer yours a wide variety, remembering to remove seeds or pits first.

who has a Ph.D. in wildlife nutrition, recently wrote an article about lory diets in *Bird Talk* magazine based on research done with rainbow lorikeets in Australia. The article addressed the fact that lorikeets do not actually need as much protein as previously thought unless the protein they are receiving is lacking in certain amino acids (the chemical building blocks of protein). A closer look at which plants have the full array of necessary amino acids, along with protein, will likely make it possible to refine a diet containing these essential proteins and no more.

Another assertion that Dr. McDonald addressed is the belief that lorikeets need a diet high in refined sugars. Just as in humans, the addition of a high percentage of refined sugar, such as honey or table sugar, creates type II diabetes in lorikeets, as well as a propensity to overindulge in these sugars. A puree of fruits and vegetables mixed with a nectar without refined sugars is actually much closer to a lory's natural diet. So, feeding the appropriate commercial nectar in addition to fruits and vegetables is very important.

Frequency of Feeding

It is not enough to feed your lory once a day and forget about it. This is one of the biggest challenges of keeping lories: your lory really should get at least two meals a day, with any food that might spoil being cleaned up a few hours

Edible Flowers

Bottlebrush (*Callistemon* spp.)

Calendula (*Calendula officinalis*)

Carnation (*Dianthus caryophyllus*)

Chamomile flowers (*Anthemis nobilis* and *Matricaria recutita*)

Chives (*Allium schoenoprasum*)

Daisies (*Bellis perennis*)

Dandelion (*Taraxacum* spp.)

Elderberry flowers (*Sambucus canadensis*)

Eucalyptus flowers (*Eucalyptus* spp.)

Gladiolus (*Gladiolus* spp.)

Hibiscus (*Hibiscus rosa-sinensis*)

Impatiens (*Impatiens walleriana*)

Lilac (*Syringa vulgaris*)

Marigold (*Tagetes patula*)

Milk thistle (*Silybum marianum*)

Nasturtiums (*Tropaeolum majus*)

Pansies (*Viola* X *wittrockiana*)

Passionflower (*Passiflora* spp.)

Roses (*Rosa* spp.)

Sage (*Salvia officinalis*)

Vegetable flowers—squash, okra, pumpkin, zucchini flowers

Violets (*Viola odorata*)

after being offered. This can make it difficult for the lory enthusiast to leave on vacation or even get away for a weekend, and it's something that you should consider before you get a lory.

You will have to decide on a feeding schedule that works for you and your lory. A reasonable feeding schedule is a meal in the morning and a meal in the afternoon. Lories may forage and eat all day long in the wild, so numerous feedings are more natural for them. Matt Schmit lists the diet at his aviary on his website www.loriinae.com. Schmit, a long-time lory breeder and a zoological professional, feeds fruit and vegetable puree in the morning and commercial nectar in the afternoon. He supplements these feedings with occasional chunks of produce and soaked pellets. He also sometimes replaces the puree with a fruit and vegetable chop that also includes brown rice, lentils, and split peas.

Live Food

It's reasonable to assume that giving lories live insects will increase their protein intake, thus making bugs a good overall addition to their diet. And lories do occasionally eat insects in the wild, although this may or may not be intentional or necessary. Certain species of lories seem to relish live insects when they are offered them during breeding season. Mealworms, wax worms, crickets, and other insects are available commercially and can be offered to lories. You can also find mixes of freeze-dried insects. However,

Leafy greens, such as spinach, mustard greens, and dandelion greens, are very healthy items to feed your lory.

neither of these are a necessary addition to a lory diet.

Water

It was once thought that water was not important to lories because they got plenty of liquid from nectar and the moist fruits in their diet. This is not the case at all! Fresh clean water should be available to all birds, at all times. This may be especially important to lories, birds who love to bathe and also love to make a soup out of everything. Water should be changed frequently, at least a couple of times a day or as soon as you notice your lory has contaminated it.

If it's challenging keeping clean water in your lory's cage, consider using drinking bottles like those used by hamsters and rabbits. However, drinking bottles should be monitored closely. If the bottle drains or the little ball that keeps the water from spilling out gets stuck, your bird may be left without access to water.

Dangerous Foods

Although a varied diet is incredibly important, you should also be careful not to feed your lory dangerous foods. The standard dangers that apply to a parrot are the same for lories: never give your lory chocolate, caffeine, or alcohol. You should also avoid salty foods or anything else that wouldn't be on a healthy diet for people. A lory is likely to try just about anything you offer him, having a propensity to test things out with his tongue, so don't give him anything you are not sure about.

There are a few things you should definitely avoid with lories in particular. The only nectars that should be given to a lory are those are designed

Grit

Grit is primarily needed by birds who eat seed. Grit allows seed-eating species to grind up hard food, and it aids in digestion. Since lories do not eat much hard food or seed, grit is not really a necessity, and they will likely ignore it if you offer it to them. So, there is no need to give lories grit.

exclusively for their consumption. Do not give them juices and nectars that are made for people. These have refined sugar, preservatives, and other things that are not healthy for lories.

You should also avoid avocados. There is some question as to whether they are poisonous to birds, but there's enough documentation of birds becoming ill and dying that it is better to be safe than sorry. Since it sometimes seems as if more foods are being added to the prohibited list every day, it's a good idea to consult a knowledgeable veterinarian if you are

My Lory Likes Sunflower Seeds

It is not unusual to hear tales of lories sneaking seeds from beneath the cages of other household parrots. A couple of seeds will not hurt them, and some lory breeders feed certain species a few seeds in their diet. It is not that seeds are harmful to these birds; it is just that seeds provide them with very little nutrition. Do not worry if your lory eats some seeds, but do not make them a significant part of his diet.

Pellets can make up part of your lory's diet, but they should not be a major component. The pellet in this photo looks like it was intended for parrots larger than lories.

uncertain about the safety of any food items.

Time-Saving Tips

With such a specialized diet, preparing a lory's daily meals can be rather labor intensive. Although this work can be pretty daunting, you can make the preparation a little less work.

If you feed your bird a "chop" of fruits and vegetables, prepare the food in advance and freeze it. If you separate the chop into containers for several days' worth of meals, you can thaw each meal portion in the refrigerator and feed it as needed, instead of prepping fresh veggies every time you feed.

You can also freeze puree. Use an ice cube tray to separate out meals. Or, freeze a few days' worth of meals and thaw them in the refrigerator, feeding as needed. Add a bit of warm water if the mixture is too thick after thawing.

Having an extra set of bowls ready to swap out can really save you time as well. It is always a good idea to have a second set, and having three or four sets of bowls is even better. This way, you always have clean bowls to swap out, even when several sets are waiting in the dishwasher.

4

Life With Lories

The more you understand about what your lory needs to stay busy and healthy on a daily the basis, the more enjoyment you will get from your new friendship. It is not enough to just feed your bird and give him the occasional new toy. Parrots are intelligent animals and need a great deal of interaction and daily care. So, before you bring your lory home, make sure you are prepared to fit your new friend into your life.

Quarantine

If you already have parrots in your home, you probably have a good idea of what you are getting into by adding one more bird to the flock. Still, there are precautions you should take. If you do have other birds in the house, definitely consider setting up a quarantine area for your new lory. Although you may have purchased your lory from a trustworthy source, there is still no guarantee that the bird you are bringing home is completely healthy. Birds are amazingly good at hiding the signs of illness. In fact, your new lory could be carrying an illness that does not become obvious until the bird has been stressed by the change in his environment. It would be very sad to have a brand new bird die from a surprise illness, but it would be tragic

Your new lory likely will be a bit apprehensive of the change in his surroundings. Be patient and gentle in your interactions with him.

to lose all of your birds because you've brought a contagious disease home with your new lory.

Ideally, a quarantined area has its own air supply. Many diseases that parrots contract are airborne. So, it's best if you can set up a new bird in a building separate from your home. Many people do not have this option, however, so although it is not ideal, you can also set up your new bird in another room in the house that is as far away from your resident birds as possible.

Be sure to take other precautions as well, such as feeding and caring for the new bird last. After you are finished, throw your clothes in the laundry, remove your shoes, take a shower, and wash your hands. You want to avoid any sort of cross-contamination until you are certain that your new lory has a clean bill of health. It's a good idea to quarantine your new bird for at least a month.

Acclimating

Once your lory comes out of quarantine, or if he is not going into quarantine, as soon as you bring him home, acclimate him to his new living environment. Make sure the first few days are quiet, to give him a chance to adjust to his new surroundings. The day you bring your bird home is probably not the best day to have a big dinner party or a birthday celebration for your nieces and nephews. Both of you should spend a bit of time simply getting to know one another in a stress-free environment.

Grapes often make a great treat for winning over the heart of a new lory. Most lories love them.

If your bird is hand-raised, he will probably be interested in interacting with you right away. Be careful to watch for signs of nervousness. If your lory moves away from you when you approach the cage, he probably is not ready to interact in a hands-on way. Give him a chance to warm up to you and learn that whenever you are around good things happen. Figure out what his favorite treats are. Many lories love grapes, and this makes them great

How Long Will My Lory Live?

Lories have not been given appropriate diets in captivity for all that long, so it's not completely certain just how long all species of lory can live. Most lories in captivity seem to live 10 to 15 years. Some species live a longer or shorter time than that, but overall, they do not live as long as other large parrots. A lifelong commitment to a lory is similar to that for a dog or a cat.

as a treat. (Too many grapes are not good for lories, so give them sparingly.) When you are acclimating your lory to interacting with you, drop a grape in his bowl when you walk by or offer him one if he will take it from your hand. Your new friend will quickly learn to look forward to your visits and will be ready to interact with you outside of his cage.

As you build your relationship, take great care that you do not do anything with your lory that might undermine your relationship. Parrots have long memories—they have to in order to survive in the wild. So, whenever you bring something

new into the house, like a big box, or do something that might be surprising, like move the couch by the parrot cage, watch your bird and make sure he is not frightened. Lories tend to be incredibly fearless, but that does not mean you shouldn't take care not to frighten your parrot.

It is also important to get your lory used to the idea of new things and to foster a willingness to investigate whatever you introduce. New food, new toys, and new activities will keep your bird's mind working and teach him to investigate and play on his own when there are new things and adventures presented to him inside his cage. If your bird is just a youngster, he will be more likely to investigate new things, so take advantage of this learning period by changing up his food and toys frequently. If you have an older bird who doesn't seem to be that interested in novel experiences, just be patient. Carefully continue to introduce new things and encourage him to explore

52   Lories and Lorikeets

and investigate. A bird who has a willingness to try new foods will be healthier. And a parrot who plays with new toys as soon as they are put in his cage is less likely to pluck himself or present other behavior problems.

Lories and Other Pets

If you have other pets in the house, it is important that you have a plan for how to manage a mixed-species household right away. Lories, perhaps more so than any other parrots, have the potential to get themselves into trouble with other pets. They are lively in their personalities, and their excitement can rapidly turn into aggression. So, make sure that your lory's cage is placed where a dog or cat cannot get a paw inside. Also consider the dangers of a lory wandering into a fish bowl, snake tank, ferret cage, or near any other pet that may be dangerous to your lory. Probably the best way to keep your lory safe is to make sure he is never anywhere near other pets. This can be very challenging, so any potential interactions between your lory and other household animals, including other parrots, should always be supervised.

It may seem as if your lory can take care of himself, but many a bird has had his beak cracked or even snapped off by a larger parrot. You should never trust your pets alone together. A cat or dog that has always gotten along with your bird may nip one day if the lory gets overexcited and delivers a sharp bite. Stories abound of dogs that have killed a bird with a surprise bite. More nerve-wracking though is a cat: It only takes one bite or scratch to cause an infection that can quickly kill your bird. If you do not see the nip or swipe happen, you may not realize that your bird needs care until it is too late. Never leave your animals unsupervised.

It is also a good idea to do some training with your other pets. A dog can be taught to put himself away in a kennel when he sees a bird on the floor. Cats are more of a challenge to train, but they can also be taught to station themselves somewhere away from the bird to wait for a treat when your lory is outside his cage. It is much better to over-think and over-plan for situations than to have to deal with tragedy.

Lory Grooming

Once you have your lory settled in and have made sure that he is safe and acclimated, you'll need to think about

No Loose Lories

Do not be tempted to leave your lory out while you go to work for the day or even just run to the grocery store. Lories can get into immense amounts of trouble in just a few moments. Even if you think you have bird-proofed your home, your lory may find a way to get himself into trouble and even danger. It is much safer to take the time to put your lory away in his cage while you are gone.

his daily, weekly, and monthly care. Although lories care for themselves in the wild, in your home they may need some help. A lory may need your assistance to make sure his feathers, beak, and nails are in perfect condition.

Wing Clipping

Wing clipping is one of the things that you should consider when you think of both your lory's grooming and his safety. There are two camps regarding clipping wings, and you will need to make up your mind what makes the most sense to you.

Clipping a bird's wings is not painful and is no different than a haircut on a person. Feathers that have grown all the way out are "dead," like human hair and fingernails. Also, clipped feathers at some point will fall out and new feathers will grow back in, so the process is not irreversible–just as a haircut is not forever.

Many people clip their parrot's wings to keep them out of as much trouble as possible. Birds who are not flighted cannot escape out of doors and windows. If your bird gets outside, there is a good chance that something terrible will happen to him if you do not get him back right away. Predators and dangerous situations abound outside the house. Parrots with well-clipped wings also cannot fly into ceiling fans or into food cooking on the stove. They are less likely to fly into rooms that they should not be in and fall into the toilet or eat a poisonous houseplant. For many parrot owners, this is a good enough reason to keep their birds clipped.

However, some small, lighter parrots seem to manage reasonable flight even with their wings clipped. And, if you plan on having your birds in an aviary, especially in a breeding situation, keeping them flighted is ideal. Even clipping a bird is not enough to guarantee its safety if you plan on taking it outside.

Like other parrots, lories preen their feathers frequently throughout the day.

Many individuals also feel that it is better for a parrot physiologically, for its heart and organs as well as its mental well-being, to be able to fly as it would in the wild. Both sides of this argument are valid, so in the end you need to make a personal decision about what is right for your parrot in your household.

If you decide it's best to clip your lory's wings, have someone with experience do it. An improper wing-clip can cause discomfort, broken feathers, and maybe even plucking. An avian veterinarian or professional bird groomer can give your bird the correct trim, and if you want to do it yourself they can teach you.

This dusky lory is fresh from his bath. Offer your lory the opportunity to bathe daily.

Feather Care

Feathers are important to a bird's well-being. Feathers will keep your lory warm in cool weather and cool in hot weather. They are the perfect clothing, but require constant care. A variety of feather types are found on a bird's body. The stiff, strong flight feathers on the wing give birds the ability to fly. Birds also have softer contour feathers on the body for climate control and protection. And they have soft, fluffy down feathers that aid in holding warmth against the body. Some down feathers even turn to powder and aid in feather care.

All of these feathers must be constantly groomed. The webbing on outer feathers must be constantly zipped back together to be effective for flight and protection. Feathers also need to be groomed to manage parasites and keep them healthy and water resistant. The powder created by powder down feathers is spread throughout the feathers, keeping them supple and water resistant. When lories and other birds care for their feathers by running their beak across feathers one by one, this is called preening. Parrots, including lories, spend a great deal of time preening, and if you have multiple birds, pairs will preen one another. This is a normal behavior in a happy, healthy bird. A bird who stops preening and whose feathers appear ragged and unkempt may be ill.

Bathing

Bathing is an important component of feather care, and this is especially true

Grooming Health Check

If you clip your lory's nails and wings on your own, be sure to do a quick health check while you have him in your hands. Thoroughly examine your bird's body for any lumps, bumps, lesions, abrasions, or discharge. Also check to make sure that your lory does not feel too thin or too plump.

of captive lories. Fed on a diet of fruit and nectar, their feathers can become soiled quickly. Most lories bathe at least once a day and often more frequently. Sticky feathers impede flight and can also be the cause of bacterial and fungal infections. A good bath is important for good health!

In the wild, lories will bathe at every opportunity they can find. They will take advantage of wet leaves after a soaking rain, puddles, and bird baths in people's gardens. Any shallow area with standing water will do. So, it is very unusual for a lory to refuse to take a bath when you offer him a bath pan. Just make sure that it is shallow and big enough so that he can open his wings and really splash. Also be prepared for everything to get soaked, because lories tend to do everything with fervor.

It is very important to offer water for bathing. Lories are so intent on the joys of feather soaking that if you do not provide a bath pan, they may choose to use their nectar for a bath. This will create a sticky mess and is certainly not good feather care. If, for some reason, your lory seems reluctant to bathe even when you do offer water, try offering wet lettuce leaves

or other greens. Your bird will likely find this irresistible and roll on his sides, flapping his wings to soak up the droplets of water.

Beak and Nail Trimming

In the wild, lories depend on their nails for hanging in branches to forage, drink, and play. Biologists have commented that lories seem to spend more time hanging upside down than they do sitting upright. This need to keep a firm grasp on the world means that lories have nails that grow rapidly, to keep them useful as they wear down. However, in captivity, their nails do not get nearly as much use

Grooming Supplies

If you are going to groom your lory at home, keep these supplies handy:

- Nail clippers
- Small blunt scissors
- Emery board
- Styptic powder

as they would in the wild. Because of this, overgrown nails are a common problem, especially in the larger species of lories.

Overgrown nails can get caught in wire welds in caging, and in toys, carpets, and furniture, as well as many other places. If a lory catches his toenail and become tangled, the toenail might break, and if breaks too close to the toe it can cause bleeding. Nails broken at the quick like this are also painful. It is best to keep your lory's toenails short enough to stop them from getting entangled, but also long enough so that they can still grasp branches firmly and retain their maneuverability. Consult your lory's breeder, veterinarian, or professional bird groomer to get instruction on how to groom your parrot's nails.

If you are uncomfortable trimming your bird's nails yourself, have an avian veterinarian or a professional bird groomer do it for you. You may be able to find a mobile grooming service to come to your home for nail trims. If you know how to do nail trimming yourself, trim the nails while the bird is wrapped in a towel, taking care not to cut too close to the quick, where the blood source lies.

Generally, your lory's beak should stay sufficiently worn down so that

For the most part, you will not have to perform any grooming of your lory's beak. However, if it starts to become overgrown, your bird needs veterinary care.

Lost Lory

If your lory accidentally gets out of the house or aviary and flies off, do not panic, even though you want to get him back immediately. If you don't know where he is, do the following:

• Post "lost parrot" flyers with his photo

• Contact local animal control and pet stores

• Put an ad in the newspaper

• List him at 911ParrotAlert.com

• Keep looking

If the information is put out right away, and to as many places as possible, many parrots are found within 24 hours.

you won't need to trim it. However, a quickly growing, overgrown upper mandible can be a sign of an underlying health problem. If your bird's beak looks as though it needs to be trimmed, take him to the vet. It is difficult to tell where the blood source on the beak begins, and a bird's beak is very sensitive. A veterinarian can make sure that the beak is trimmed without doing any harm to the lory and that the overgrown beak is not a sign of some other health problem.

On the Move

One of the challenges of living with lories is that even if you cannot be there every day to make sure your lory gets what he needs, your lory will still need daily care. You must consider what you will do when you are traveling—whether it is with or without your bird. You can expect to live with your lory for quite some time, so you should also consider what you will do if you have to move. Having an advance plan for these issues will save you a lot of trouble when the time comes for a vacation or a change of careers.

Traveling

Many hotels and vacation destinations allow pets. If you cannot stand the idea of having a fun vacation without your parrot party pal, bringing your lory along may be an option. First, make sure that your lory is comfortable in a carrier or a travel cage before you run off on a road trip. Take your lory on short trips first, and get him used to riding along for longer periods of time. This will also give you an opportunity to figure out how to best position his cage or carrier so that your bird remains safe and comfortable and your car remains fairly clean.

If you are going to travel out of state, make sure that you have a health certificate for your bird. If you get stopped somewhere and there is any question about your bird, it is best to have documentation to prove he is healthy. If you are flying, this is a necessity. If you do plan on transporting your bird on an airline, be sure to talk with someone experienced in transporting birds to find out the best airline to use and their regulations. Check in advance to see if there are any restrictions on bringing birds into the states you will be visiting as well. Occasionally, restrictions are in place to control the spread of avian diseases.

You will also want to bring fruit, nectar mix, bottled water, and any other goodies you feed your parrot. Just do not overfill bowls while traveling or you will have a sticky mess. Another challenge will be keeping all of your lory's food fresh, so bring an ice chest or cooler and plan on staying where you can conveniently mix nectar and clean bowls. Don't forget to also bring plenty of toys.

Although having a flock of lories can be fun, it may make it more challenging to find a pet sitter or to find a new place if you have to move.

Boarding and Bird Sitters

Of course, bringing your lory with you may not be ideal, especially if you are going on a vacation to get a break from everything—including pet care. If you have multiple lories, it may not even be a possibility. In this case, you will need to find either a place to board your bird or a bird sitter to come to your home.

Boarding your parrot may be the easiest thing to do if you only have one bird and no other pets. Ideally, taking your bird to a trustworthy friend who has no birds would be the best situation. You want to be careful that, wherever your bird goes, he is unlikely to pick up any diseases from other birds. If the best available choice for you is a place that specifically boards parrots, make sure that they require health certificates from all their birds. Also be sure to visit the place first and ask for a tour, making sure the bird room is clean and that the staff seems knowledgeable.

If you have multiple pets, you may find that the best

choice is to have a pet sitter come to your home. If you have a friend who has experience in caring for birds, then you are in good shape. Just make sure they are clear on how to care for your bird, have the number of your avian vet, and are familiar with your birds. If you don't have any friends who are willing to help out or who are comfortable caring for parrots, hire a professional. Make sure to interview your pet sitter before hiring her. Make sure she has experience with parrots and that she understands what to do in the event of an emergency. Also check to see if she has references–and definitely call those references.

Moving

The fact that you may have to move at some point is an important issue to consider. Many people who start with one parrot quickly find themselves enamored and soon have a growing flock. Where you live now might have room for three messy lories, but will the next place you live in allow multiple birds? Will you be able to take your lory with you if you have to move into an apartment, instead of the house you are living in now? For the most part, moving parrots from one home to another is not a problem. A change of scenery is great for parrots. Just make sure that you will be able to take your birds with you wherever you go before you add additional lories to your flock.

If you do find that you need to move, the most important thing you can do is prepare in advance. If your move is far, make sure that you will have everything you need once you and your bird arrive. Locate the closest trustworthy avian veterinarian. Find out where the best bird supply stores are in your soon-to-be home town, or figure out the best way to get things online and in the mail. Quickly identify someone to whom you can give a key to your home and instructions on how to care for your lory in case of an emergency. Make sure that all of the things your bird might need are lined up in advance in the place to which you are moving.

What Are These Little Flies?

If you feed your lories a good diet with lots of fresh fruit, chances are you are going to at some time—if not all the time—have an issue with fruit flies. Fruit flies feed on—you guessed it—fruit and they are harmless. However, they seem to appear spontaneously whenever there is plenty of fruit around. Keep things as clean as possible to keep them at bay. You can also check online for some very simple and safe homemade traps to help control the infestation.

Multi-Bird Households

Lories can be an extremely difficult pet to add to a household of multiple birds. Certainly, there is the occasional lory who gets along with everyone, and there is never a problem with aggression between birds. However, this is the exception rather than the rule. Lories more often than not are aggressive toward other birds. If you are going to have multiple birds, including a lory, loose in your home, they will require constant supervision. It is not a good idea to get a lory just so another parrot in the household has company.

Decide where your lory cage is going to go in advance, and how you are going to set it up. If you have movers traveling with your things, you may prefer to move your birds' cages yourself, rather than let movers handle it. If their cage won't fit in your car, you may need to rent a van for the move. Try to have everything set up and ready to go before your birds arrive in their new home. The more prepared you are to get right back into the normal routine, the easier things will be for both you and your lory. Hopefully, once you have a routine for day-to-day living with a lory, life will be smooth sailing. However, it is still important to be prepared for problems. Recognizing potential lory health issues is another vital aspect of caring for lories, and this is addressed in the next chapter.

5

The Healthy Lory

Generally speaking, lories who are fed an excellent diet, given fresh water, get plenty of exercise, and live in a clean environment should remain healthy. Parrots are a very hardy group of birds if care is taken to meet their needs. However, just as with any pet, lories can have accidents or get unexpected illnesses. Lories can potentially succumb to any of the diseases with which the parrot family struggles. So, it is extremely important to be able to identify when your bird is under the weather and to be prepared to deal with illness or accidents. Advance preparation could save your bird's life.

Finding a Veterinarian

The most important way to start this preparation is to find an excellent avian veterinarian. When it comes to birds, not all veterinarians are created equal. There is a lot to learn when it comes to avian medicine. In fact, there is more to learn every year. So, the best veterinarian to help you with your lory is one who is dedicated to staying current on avian medicine.

The best place to start looking for a veterinarian who specializes in avian medicine is at the website of the Association of Avian Veterinarians (www.aav.org). You can also check the American Board of Veterinary Practitioners (ABVP) for veterinarians certified in avian practice. Certified veterinarians have received further education to become specialists. Go to www.abvp.com and search under "find a diplomate" for avian veterinarians in your area.

If you happen to live in an area where no one specializes in birds, ask around. There is probably a vet in your area whom other parrot enthusiasts frequent. And, even when dealing with a veterinarian who specializes in birds, a good recommendation goes a long way. If others have had a good experience with a particular veterinarian, you likely will as well. Find a good veterinarian as soon as possible after you get your lory, or even before you bring your bird home. In an emergency, the last thing you want to worry about is whether you are taking you sick friend to a proficient vet.

Well-Checks

A good way to get to know your veterinarian and to head off any

It's best to take your lory to a veterinarian who specializes in avian medicine.

health issues that may be rearing their ugly heads is to take your parrot in for annual exams. In an annual well-check, your veterinarian will physically examine your bird to make sure he isn't over- or underweight; that his skin, mouth, and eyes look normal; that his heart and lungs sound good; and that his overall appearance is healthy. Your veterinarian may also do blood work and a fecal exam, checking for signs of illness or parasites. Even if your bird seems to be behaving normally and looks healthy, he may be hiding illness. An annual exam will give you the reassurance that your bird has a clean bill of health and will give your bird a better chance of getting well if he does have something wrong.

Taking your bird in once a year or so also allows you to get to know your veterinarian better and to find out if there is anything new in the world of avian medicine and nutrition that you should be aware of. You can also have your lory's wings and nails clipped if you prefer to not do this yourself.

If your lory is sitting with his eyes closed and his feathers fluffed up for long periods of time, he could be ill. A musk lorikeet is shown here.

Signs of Trouble

Even if you take your lory in for a periodic check-up, you should still know the signs of sickness in a bird. Generally speaking, if your bird looks ill in any way, get him to the veterinarian right away. Once a parrot exhibits obvious signs of illness, he is probably a very sick bird.

Watch for any behavioral changes in your bird. Lories are lively and active, and most are vocal. Like all birds, they will settle in for a nap now and again, but if your lory seems unusually sedate for a long period of time, there may be a problem. If your bird is not interested in his normal food, especially if he ignores his favorite treats, get him to the veterinarian immediately. Take note if he is not drinking water or is drinking water excessively. Once you get to know your lory's normal behavior, you should be able to easily notice when something is amiss. So, learn what is normal for your bird as quickly as possible.

Watch for physical signs that your lory is not feeling well. If you bird is sitting quietly with his feathers fluffed up and eyes closed and is not just taking a nap, he is probably ill. Any discharge from the eyes or nostrils, and any swelling, is a sign that something is wrong. Debris and feces caked around the vent or the underside of the tail are also a sign of sickness.

Emergency Care

Having an emergency kit can be extremely helpful for quick triage before you get to the veterinarian or for stabilizing your bird if you cannot get him to the veterinarian right away. It is a bad idea to "wait and see" if your lory is going to get better. However, if it is the middle of the night or a holiday, and you have no emergency vet to go to, you should at least have a place to keep your bird warm and calm until you can get him professional care.

When to See the Vet

If you see any of the following, take your lory to the veterinarian right away:

• Difficulty breathing

• Excessive bleeding

• Listlessly sitting on floor of cage puffed up

• Open wound

• Seizure

The Hospital Cage

Warmth is vital to sick birds. Set up a hospital cage, made of an empty aquarium or a small cage, with a heating pad underneath only one side to keep your lory warm; if your bird gets too warm, he can move over to the other, cooler side. Cover the hospital cage with towels. All birds have a difficult time maintaining their body temperature when they are fluffed up and ill, so isolating your bird in a warm, small cage will help. Just be sure to check periodically to make sure he is not too hot.

Common Emergencies

It is helpful to be familiar with some of the common pet bird emergencies so that you can calmly handle the situation and get your bird to the veterinarian safely and without further injury. Here are a few of the most common mishaps.

Broken Blood Feather

Sometimes lories will break a *blood feather*, a feather that is still growing in and has a blood supply. These feathers are the larger, stiffer feathers in the wings or tail, and they may be damaged if a lory is startled and breaks it against his cage. If the feather continues to bleed, use styptic powder or corn starch to clot the bleeding as soon as possible and without panicking the lory. The styptic power may sting, so it is best to secure your bird in a towel, get the bleeding to clot, and wait a bit before you release him.

The feather may begin to bleed again if your lory knocks it against something or preens away the clotted blood. If this happens, the feather may need to be extracted. It is best to have a veterinarian or someone experienced at feather removal do this. Plucking the feather can damage the follicle and the feather may grow back damaged or not grow back at all.

Example of blood feathers on an Amazon parrot. Those on lories look similar. Broken blood feathers bleed and require immediate attention.

Wounds and Bites

The exuberant curiosity of lories has gotten many a household parrot into trouble. It is always a lory owner's responsibility to know where her lory is at all times and to be aware of any trouble that he might get himself into. Still, lories may end up underfoot, injure themselves by getting into areas they shouldn't, and also be bit or scratched by other pets.

If you find that your lory has a cut, clean it out and stop the bleeding right away. Again, you may have to gently wrap your bird in a towel to keep him from injuring himself further. Cleaning the wound with hydrogen peroxide will flush things out until you can get your bird to the veterinarian.

If your bird has been bit or scratched, stop the bleeding, clean out the wound if it is superficial, and get

him to your veterinarian right away. Do not wait! This is a true emergency for birds, as your lory can go quickly into shock. Bite wounds usually need surgical repair, and if the bite was from a small mammal, especially a cat, your bird is in grave danger. Many cats carry oral *Pasteurella multocida*, which is a dangerous bacteria. Even if your bird seems fine, he will need to be treated with antibiotics as a preventative measure.

Feathers are excellent at covering up bite marks. It isn't unusual for a lory to get bit, but have his owner be unable to find the wound. A bitten parrot seems fine for a while, but will quickly succumb to infection if not treated. So, if your lory has a run-in with a dog or cat, get him to his veterinarian immediately.

First-Aid Kit Contents

- Antibiotic ointment
- Rubbing alcohol
- Bandages and gauze
- Cotton balls
- Cotton swabs
- Hydrogen peroxide
- Styptic powder
- Tweezers

Fractures

Fractures or broken bones are not uncommon and are usually easy to identify. Only a small amount of soft tissue surrounds the bones on birds, so breaks often appear as open wounds. Bird bones, although sturdy, can break easily because the bone is porous and hollow to aid in flight.

If you notice that your lory is not bearing weight on one foot or has a drooping wing, inspect it closely. It may be broken. If so, get your bird in a carrier or box where he can sit comfortably without stressing himself further and take him to the vet. Lories with broken bones may go into shock and need fluids, treatment for potential infections, and to have the bone set so that it heals in the correct position.

Poisoning

Poisoning is another common household bird disaster. Lories tend to investigate everything with their tongues and if they find something toxic, they may accidentally poison themselves. This makes it incredibly important to bird-proof your home. If your bird looks under the weather and you are uncertain why he may be ill, be sure to look around the house before you take him to the veterinarian. You may find some evidence that your bird has gotten into something toxic. This sort of information will help your veterinarian quickly help your bird.

If your bird gets into a toxic cleaning agent, nail polish remover, a poisonous plant, a glass of alcohol, or chocolate, he will quickly become ill. If you catch him in the act, determine if your bird has actually consumed any of the poison and call your veterinarian right away. Then, take your lory in if your veterinarian recommends it. Your vet may be able to give your bird something to absorb or flush out the toxin.

Some poisonings, such as zinc or lead toxicity, happens gradually and a poisoned bird will slowly begin presenting vague signs of illness. Avoid any toys, quick links, or cage materials that may be made with lead or zinc.

Egg Binding

Just because your female bird lives alone does not mean she will not lay an egg. It is a good idea to have your bird sexed the first time you take her to the vet so you can be aware of whether or not egg binding might be an issue. DNA sexing is nonintrusive and fairly inexpensive. Your veterinarian can send off a blood or feather sample to be tested to find out definitively whether or not your lory is a male or a female.

Hens can have a variety of dangerous or even deadly issues surrounding the production and laying of eggs. Egg binding occurs when a bird is unable to pass an egg. There are a variety of reasons for this including, but certainly not limited to, obesity, malnutrition, calcium deficiency, excessive egg production, stress, old age, and being a first-time egg layer. If a lory is unable to pass an egg for a long period of time, she will die. It is very important that you recognize the symptoms of egg binding and get her appropriate treatment.

An egg-bound bird will exhibit signs of "depression." She may sit fluffed up on the floor of her cage. She may demonstrate a loss of appetite and energy. You may also notice her straining and wagging her tail and standing with a wide stance as she tries

Many houseplants are toxic. Carefully supervise your lory whenever he is out of his cage to prevent him from ingesting anything toxic.

Egg Laying

If your lory lays eggs, it may be best to just let her sit on them (or *brood* them) for a while. She will probably only sit on them for a couple of weeks before she gets bored and abandons them. As soon as you notice that she is no longer interested in her eggs, remove them. If you take the eggs away while she's still sitting on them, she may simply lay two more. Laying excessive numbers of eggs can increase the possibility of her becoming egg bound. She is more likely only to lay eggs a couple of times a year if you do not take them away until she has finished brooding.

to pass the egg. You may or may not be able to feel the egg in the oviduct at the base of her tail, but take her to the veterinarian even if you don't feel an egg. Your vet will take an x-ray to see exactly what is going on. Your bird may need surgery to collapse and remove the egg.

Dietary Problems

The most common issues that avian veterinarians encounter in their lory patients are dietary problems. Improper feeding can lead to disease, including seizures. Hopefully, having read Chapter 3, you are giving your lory the best possible diet. But it's likely that asking what you feed your parrot will be one of your veterinarian's first questions. It is a good idea to bring along a list of what you feed to give to your veterinarian.

Dietary issues may be caused by an excess of vitamins and minerals, not just a deficiency. An increasingly

identified dietary disorder in lories is hemochromatosis, also called iron storage disease. Iron is normally stored in the liver and used to produce hemoglobin. Lories who are fed a diet too high in iron may store excess iron, to the point of toxicity. Hemochromatosis can cause death; it is usually asymptomatic, and only discovered when a necropsy is done to determine why a bird died. It is incredibly important to feed foods that are produced specifically for lories and are low in iron. Avoiding feeding anything like baby food, juices, and nectars enriched with iron. Talk to your vet to see what she recommends.

Bacterial Infections

Bacteria are naturally occurring organisms present in all environments. Generally, a lory will not get a bacterial infection as long as he lives in a clean environment, is provided with fresh food and water, and his body is not otherwise compromised in any way. Bacteria can flourish in a bird's body when he is sick with something else or suffering from stress. If a particularly virulent bacterium is introduced into an environment or your lory is already under the weather, he may get an infection.

Your veterinarian will do a culture to determine if your bird has a bacterial infection and he will check to see if the bacterium is resistant to any antibiotics, so that she can prescribe the most effective medication. If you have multiple birds, consider your ill lory contagious and treat him as if in quarantine. Also take care to wash your hands and not touch food or your mouth after handling your lory. Potential bacterial infections include *E. coli*, *Salmonella*, and *Mycobacterium* (avian tuberculosis) among others, and some of these can be transmitted to humans.

Psittacosis

Psittacosis is one of the bacteria (*Chlamydiaphila psittaci*) that can be transmitted to humans; the illness it causes is often referred to as *parrot fever*. People who contract this disease from their birds are almost always immune-suppressed, which means that a healthy person is very unlikely to be infected by her birds. In humans, this bacterial infection presents similarly to the flu. In parrots, the symptoms include lethargy, difficulty breathing, and discolored droppings. The infection can be treated with antibiotics when diagnosed, but all birds in the household must be treated and all areas and objects that the birds come in contact with must be thoroughly disinfected.

Fungal Infections

Fungus, like bacteria, is normally present in the environment and even in our bodies. Fungus only turns into an

Dietary and nutritional issues are the most common problems seen in pet lories. Feeding too much seed is just one possible cause of nutritional disorders.

infection when it begins to grow out of control and harms the body. There are two ways to prevent fungal infections. One is to keep the environment as free of fungus as possible. The liquid quality of lory diets often encourages the growth of fungus, so keeping things clean is very important. The other way to keep lories from getting fungal infections is to keep them healthy. A lory with a compromised immune system is more likely to succumb to a fungal infection than is a healthy bird.

Aspergillosis

Aspergillus is a common fungus in most environments and is especially prevalent in damp, unventilated areas. In small doses, the fungus is harmless; it is only a danger when allowed to grow in large quantities, where a bird can breathe in the spores.

When a lory contracts an *Aspergillus* infection, it is called *aspergillosis* and can be very difficult to manage. The fungus grows in the respiratory system, causing breathing difficulty, exhaustion, weight loss, and often death. It can be a difficult disease to treat once it takes hold, and even with an antifungal treatment, the bird may not recover. Prevention is important. Avoid using corn cobs and other bedding materials that can stay damp and become a ready home to *Aspergillus.*

Candidiasis

Yeast (*Candida*) is another common fungus in the environment that can become the source of digestive tract, mouth, and respiratory infections. Yeast is normally found within the body, but when yeast takes hold to the level of being considered an infection it is called *candidiasis* (or thrush). Generally, candidiasis is a secondary problem that is caused because of some underlying illness. If your lory is stressed, undernourished, or sick with another disease, the

Oh no! My Lory Is Losing all His Feathers

It is normal for a lory to lose or molt his feathers every year. At certain times of the year, it might seem as if your lory is exploding, but he likely will not lose all his feathers. All birds grow in new feathers every year, to replace worn and faded plumage. If your lory seems to be actually plucking out feathers in a particular spot, however, take him to his vet right away.

If you have multiple birds, quarantine any who come down with a bacterial infection to avoid it spreading through your flock.

yeast that naturally occurs in his body may begin to multiply unchecked and cause problems. Frequently, candidiasis is caused by using antibiotics, which kill those bacteria that normally keep naturally occurring yeast at much lower levels in the body.

A lory who has a yeast infection may have a whitish build-up around his beak and mouth. He will also be listless and look ill. Unlike aspergillosis, candidiasis is fairly easily treated if caught early enough. Your veterinarian can determine the presence of an infection with a fecal gram stain and treat it with an antifungal.

Parasites

Parasites feed off the blood or other nutrients in a host animal's body. They are a common problem for all birds, and generally do not pose health issues unless they become an infestation. If a bird is overinfested with parasites, he may give up all of his nutrients to the freeloading parasites, thus becoming weak and ill. However, parasites are very easy to prevent and to treat.

Mites and Lice

Mites and lice are very common in aviaries. Wild birds almost always carry mites and lice and can easily pass them on to the birds in your aviary. For the most part, these parasites are not dangerous, but they can be itchy and uncomfortable. Some lice are species specific, but others can be found on almost any bird. You can see some kinds of lice and mites as tiny specks moving through the feathers; others can only be seen under a microscope.

If your bird seems to be preening excessively, or if you can see lice or mites on his feathers, eliminate these pests as soon as possible. Many miticidal sprays are available at pet stores and bird suppliers; just follow the directions carefully when you spray your bird and his affected area. If you have multiple birds, be sure to treat them all.

Coccidiosis

Coccidiosis is the name for a variety of protozoal parasites that can live in the intestines of birds, including lories. If your lory has a coccidiosis infection, she may seem lethargic. She will lose weight, and her droppings may not look normal. Lories can die from coccidiosis if it goes untreated.

A vet can diagnose this parasite and treat it easily. Most pet lories will not have a problem with this parasitic infection, but it is extremely common in wild birds. Indoor birds are less likely to contract an infection, but birds in an outdoor aviary should be checked periodically for coccidiosis.

Psittacine Beak and Feather Disease

Psittacine beak and feather disease (PBFD) is a virus that was first described in the 1970s. It causes deformities in feathers and beak and also feather loss. Most parrots who contracted PBFD ultimately died. For some time, it was recommended that birds testing positive for PBFD be euthanized.

Recently, scientists have identified a different strain of PBFD, which they are differentiating with the name PBFD 2. It has been found only in lories thus far. PBFD is not uncommon in captive lories and is common in wild lorikeets in Australia. In a study of affected birds in the 1980s in Australia, almost

Stress

Stress in one of the biggest causes of illness. Stress can occur for a variety of reasons. If two lories are housed together and one is an aggressive bird, the less aggressive bird is likely to be stressed. Housing birds next to noises or lights that do not allow them to rest, or even placing them next to an area that makes them feel vulnerable to danger can be stressful. Watch your lory to make sure he seems comfortable and confident. A lory who is constantly stressed is likely to become ill.

Housing different species of lories together can cause stress to the less aggressive birds. This will make them more susceptible to a variety of illnesses.

half of the birds studied recovered from the disease within one or two molts. It is possible that they had this less-virulent strain of PBFD. This is still a very frightening disease, but if your bird is diagnosed with PBFD, there is a possibility that she may recover from the virus. This is another instance of why it is so vitally important to have a veterinarian dedicated to keeping current with the rapidly changing information available in the world of avian medicine.

Summing up

Quarantining and vet-checking new birds can prevent the spread of disease when you bring a new lory into your home. The best way to avoid infections and illnesses is to keep your lory's cage, play area, and toys as clean as possible. Make sure his food is always fresh, and remove it before it spoils. If you have an aviary, do not let it get overcrowded. Good care and cleaning will go a long way toward keeping your lory or lories healthy.

6

Lory
Behavior
and
Training

Understanding your lory and working to build a strong relationship are critical to enjoying your new friend. The first thing you must understand is that lories are not little people. If you think of them as human, you may misjudge the reasons for their behavior, which will only encourage behavioral problems. Enjoy your lory for his "lory-ness." They are smart, interactive, and almost always good for a laugh. They bring so much to your home!

Also, keep in mind that lories are wild animals who have not been bred for house manners and appropriate interactions. Lories have not been selectively bred for their temperament, as domestic animals have been. Dogs and cats have been bred to fit into our lives, but lories are only a couple of generations removed from the wild. What your lory does is pretty close to what he would be doing in his native habitat. So, the least you can do is help your lory stay active while he figures out the best ways to get your attention and fit into his new human household.

Natural History
One of the most important steps in having a well-behaved parrot is finding out everything you can about his

Learning about your lory's behavior in the wild will help you understand his behavior in your home.

natural history. Where a parrot lives, what he eats, when he breeds, and how he interacts with his environment overall will help you understand why he acts the way he does in your home. Understanding what his natural behaviors are will help you "translate" the things he does.

Read everything you can about the species of lory that you bring into your home. Talk to breeders of that particular species and anyone who might have seen them in the wild. If a nearby zoo has a lory exhibit, visit it so that you can watch lories interact with one another. If you have a rainbow lorikeet, you will find a tremendous amount of video on YouTube of lorikeets in Australia frolicking in people's gardens and bird baths. All of these things will help you understand the sometimes strange and always fascinating behavior of your lory.

Body Language

If you are new to lories, and especially if you are new to parrots, your bird's body language may be very difficult for you to understand. Reading birds does not come naturally to most of us. They don't have bony tails to wag or swish their disapproval, as dogs and cats do. They do not have teeth to bare when they are afraid or about to bite. They still have plenty of ways to show you what they mean, but feathers are a lot harder for us humans to read. So, it is very important that you pay attention and learn to "read" your lory.

Keep It Short

Parrots have short attention spans, and with lories this can be especially true. Fruit-eating birds also have small appetites, so if you are training with food, your lory may fill up quickly. Regardless of why your lory loses interest during training, it is important that you end your training session before he does. Keep these sessions short: Sometimes just a couple of minutes is plenty.

Lory body language tends to be pretty "big." Lories do everything enthusiastically, so in some ways they can be easier to read than other parrots. An excited lory may bob his head with fervor and tap a foot. He might expand and contract his pupils, "pinning" his eyes. You might also see him arch his neck, with the feathers fluffed. These are all signs of excitement and are easy to identify. Unfortunately, an enthusiastic lory can rapidly move from excited to aggressive. Trying to handle a highly excited lory is likely to get you bit. So, it helps to learn to read the nuances of your bird's body language.

You should also learn to watch for body language that demonstrates that your bird is nervous or fearful. It is very important that you keep your relationship with your bird positive at all times. The fewer negative experiences your lory has with you, the stronger your relationship will be.

Training Techniques That Don't Work

Using these techniques to get your lory to stop doing something may undermine your relationship:

• Flicking his beak

• Squirting him with water

• Shaking his cage

• Throwing things at his cage

• Yelling at him

Keep in mind that yelling at your lory is actually rewarding. Lories love a ruckus and often do not understand that you are yelling at them. Water-loving lories may also enjoy being sprayed with water, so again you may get the opposite effect from what you intended.

So, if your bird moves to the back of the cage, leans away, or tries to fly away when you approach, back off and approach again more slowly or at a later time. Fortunately, lories do not tend to be fearful birds–plenty of lorikeet videos on the Internet show wild lorikeets mobbing people who are willing to feed them. Unlike some parrots, neither do lories tend to be nervous by nature. A lory who is comfortable with you and his surroundings will approach you willingly, sit with a foot up and feathers relaxed, and spend time interacting with his environment. However, every bird is an individual, so learn to read your lory's body and respond appropriately.

Positive Reinforcement

When working with parrots, it makes a huge difference when you use positive reinforcement and avoid all negative interactions. Positive reinforcement simply means paying attention to things you like or want your parrot to do and then rewarding him for them. Parrots do not respond well to punishment, and trying to change bad behavior by punishing them is never as effective as encouraging good behavior by using praise and treats. By rewarding a behavior, you increase the likelihood that the bird will repeat it. And if you ignore bad behavior, it will likely diminish if not stop all together.

Aversive punishment and negative reinforcement should be avoided when interacting with your lory. In simple terms, this means that you should not use things your parrot does not like and tries to avoid in order to train him. This can be as minor as pushing on the back of a parrot's legs with a stick to get him to step up. Your bird will step up in order to get you to stop pushing him with the stick, but using training techniques that force a parrot to do something can be counterproductive or at least not very effective; this is especially obvious with a bird as energetic as a lory.

Instead, if you train your bird with positive reinforcement, such as offering a treat for stepping up on a perch, your lory will get to make his own decision and be rewarded for making the right choice. The great side effect of this is that an animal who gets a reward for doing something he is asked to do is likely to be creative and work harder to find other ways to get your attention and treats. You clearly communicate in a positive way, and your bird is able to make his own choices and control his behavior. Understanding positive reinforcement is the most important tool in your arsenal when you are trying to communicate with your parrot.

Consistency

In addition to keeping your interactions positive, consistency is another critical tool in training a well-behaved lory. Understand that every time you interact with your lory in any way—stopping to talk to him, playing with him, or giving him a treat—you are communicating to him that whatever he was doing when he got your attention is something that you wanted. After all, you rewarded him. Be consistent about your message, and only reward those behaviors you like or at least don't mind. Since we cannot sit down with our parrots and explain the rules of the household to them or expect them to figure it out intuitively, the way our dogs do, it is critical that your message be clear.

Many people accidentally train

Pay attention to your lory's posture, his feather position, and the movement of his pupils to determine his level of excitement.

their parrots to engage in bad behavior because they do not realize they are rewarding it. If your lory is screaming at the top of his lungs, now is not a good time to offer him a treat. You may think that having a mouthful of food will quiet him down, but what your lory understands from this interaction is that when he screams you come running with a treat. Think about what you are communicating to your bird and then be consistent. Consistency is a great communication tool. If you never pick up, feed, or interact with your lory when he is screaming, he has no reason to think that making a ruckus is what is expected of him or the best way to get some one-on-one time.

If your bird leans away from being touched, respect his wishes and try working with him a little later.

Taming

Fortunately, hand-raised lories are readily available and they arrive ready to interact with you. And even wild lories tame rapidly, becoming accustomed to and comfortable with interacting with people rapidly. If you do bring home a lory who is not comfortable stepping up, letting you scratch him, or playing with you, then take note from the lories in the wild. The best way to get them to happily land on people's hands and enjoy "people time" is to use patience and positive reinforcement.

If you have a lory who is not ready to be best friends right away, start by simply training him to interact with you. The most important thing to understand when working with a new parrot is that every interaction is a training session. You are teaching your bird what to expect from you. This makes taming the most important training of all. While taming your bird, you teach him that you are trustworthy, respectful, and a worthy friend.

Some of the older ideas of taming a parrot involve getting him on the floor where he is uncomfortable and afraid and then getting him to step up onto your hand where he would theoretically be more comfortable. Other methods involve cornering a bird and handling him until he gets "used" to you. Neither of these methods is the best choice for taming. Building a relationship based on putting the bird in uncomfortable positions and forcing him to "get over" his fear of you and his environment does not build a solid base for a good relationship. You are likely to get bit, and your parrot is not going to find the experience enjoyable either.

So, rather than force him to get over his fear of you by spending a lot of time around him or trying to immediately handle him, instead teach him that he should look forward to seeing you. Start by figuring out what he likes best as a treat. If you have a parrot who is nervous when you approach, then simply drop a treat in his bowl and walk away. Your parrot will soon learn that seeing you coming means he's about to get a treat. When your parrot moves to the front of the cage when he sees you coming and waits for the imminent treat, then you're ready to go to the next step.

In small steps, work toward getting your bird to take a treat from your fingers, thus using positive reinforcement to teach him that being touched is a positive thing. Begin working on building his confidence in being near your hands, encouraging him with a treat in one hand to get a little closer to the fingers of your other hand. Always watch his body language, making sure that he is confident with each step, and keep your sessions short. A good length of time for a training session is about five or ten minutes.

Once he is comfortable being near your hands, gently touch him as he's reaching for the treat and say "good." Watch to make sure he isn't uncomfortable. Move slowly and give your bird the option to move away if he doesn't want to be touched. Eventually, he will decide that if a light touch gets him a treat, there's no harm in it. And as he gets more and more comfortable with being touched, he will learn that a good scratch from a human with skilled fingers is its own reward. If you spend time taming your new parrot, you will both be more confident with one another and have laid a great groundwork for any further training that you do. Of course, with lories, taming often happens very quickly, but

Food rewards are useful tools for training and taming parrots. Use a small piece of one of your lory's favorite treats.

Event Markers

An event marker is a noise that marks the moment at which your lory has done what you asked and lets him know exactly what you are rewarding. A clicker can be used as an event marker and so can a word like "good." The important thing is that your event marker is short and fast. You need it to mark the exact moment the bird did the right thing in order to help him understand what you are training.

it's still a good idea to take the time to keep it positive.

Behavior Basics

Once you have a bird who enjoys interacting with you and who you feel comfortable with, you can train some very simple behaviors that will help build your relationship throughout your lory's life. Training does not have to include silly parlor tricks. Training can simply be teaching your parrot to do things that will help him in everyday life.

But there's nothing wrong with tricks, either! If you have fun training your lory to play basketball with a miniature ball and hoop, there's nothing demeaning about that. Any time that you spend with your bird interacting in a positive way is a benefit to your lory. Parrots of all species are intelligent and love to have problems to solve and activities in which to engage. When you train your bird, you give him a constructive way to engage his brain, directing his fun instead of giving him an opportunity to find new kinds of mischief.

Step Up

One of the most basic things to train–and one of the most helpful–is the *step-up*. We, of course, want our birds to step up when we ask. Usually, we ask because we need to move them for a reason. The important thing is that we ask. The idea that parrots "must" step-up when asked has forced many a parrot lover to deal with a biting parrot. It has also created a great many parrots who are hand-shy and nervous around hands that might at any moment be shoved underneath them and push them around. It is much more effective to teach a parrot that, when he is asked to step up, he will likely get something he wants for complying.

First figure out what your lory is most likely to accept for a treat. Then, offer your hand for your bird to step up on and offer a treat with the other hand. Start by trying to get your lory to reach over your hand to get a treat. If he seems comfortable and confident with reaching over your hand, then hold the next treat far enough away so that he has to place one foot on your hand to lean over and get the treat. When you do this, say "step up"; when his foot touches your hand, say "good" and give him the treat. In this way, you are making it clear that he is being rewarded for placing his foot on your hand.

From this point, ask him to progress in small steps. First, one foot just touching your hand. Then, adjust your criteria for saying "good" and giving a treat to putting one foot solidly on your hand–then both feet. Then, have your bird step up and wait for two seconds. Then, maybe move your hand a bit and reward him.

All of the time, you want to make sure that your lory is comfortable. If he leans back and wants to step off your hand, let him. You are trying to teach him that you are trustworthy, that stepping up is his decision, and that there are great rewards once he understands what you are asking him and chooses to do it.

Stick Training

You may also want to train the *step up* to a dowel or a perch. When your lory is overly excited, but you need to pick him up, replacing your hand with a wooden perch might save you from getting bit. It will also help if someone

It is important to train your bird to step up because this will allow you to move him when you need to.

Clicker Training

Clickers are a wonderful way to train. Using a clicker as an event marker (the sound lets the parrot know a reward is coming) is very precise. You can find clickers at most pet stores, as they are often used to train dogs and many other types of animals. The Resources section of this book lists a few good clicker training websites. If you find that using a clicker works well for you, go for it!

has to take care of your lory but isn't comfortable picking him up. Train the *step up* the same way, only replace your hand with a perch. Be sure to get lots of repetitions with treats and do refresher training now and then so that your lory continues to see stepping up on the perch as a positive.

Stationing

Another easy thing to train your bird—and a behavior that can keep him out of all kinds of mischief—is *stationing*. Training animals to station is a common husbandry technique used in zoos. If you need to work with an animal that is dangerous or uncomfortable being touched, teaching him to go to a particular place for a reward can help you get close enough to examine him or move him to a secure place away from the zookeeper. You can use this same technique to send your lory someplace safe if there is trouble, or if you just want to keep him out of mischief.

Stationing can be very helpful to keep parrots off the floor and stop them from attacking feet. First, choose a spot for your bird to station and stay

for a reward. The top of a play stand or cage can be great for this. Mark the spot with a nontoxic marker or a piece of nontoxic tape. Choose a word to cue this behavior, like "station" or something else short and easy. Then begin training.

Place your lory next to the spot, first making sure he is not nervous of the modifications you've made. If he is comfortable say, "station" and hold a treat just far enough away from the spot that he has to step on it in order to get the treat. As soon as he steps on it say, "good" and let him have the reward. He will likely move away from it again to finish he treat. Once he's finished, try to get him to station again. After you've done this a few times, you'll see him "get it."

When he starts deliberately stepping on the station, ask him to step up, move him a little further away from it, and then ask him to "station" again. Make sure you train in small increments to ensure that he understands and does not get frustrated. Once you have him trained to station though, you should be able to get him to climb up the cage and walk over to his spot when you give him the cue. You will also find that he spontaneously stations, hoping for treat. As long as you often reward him with attention or treats when you see him on his station spot, he will continue to offer this behavior. Training your lory to find his way to a safe spot to get what he wants can save you a lot of headaches and maybe even your lory's life.

Targeting

Targeting is another simple training exercise that can help you with a lory who is getting into or about to get into trouble. It will also help if you think that your wound-up lory might take a swipe at you. *Targeting* can be completely hands off and is much like *stationing*, except that you can move the target you want your lory to touch.

First, select the object you will use for a target. A chopstick with the tip dyed in food coloring works well for a target. They are easy to get, easy to replace if they break, and easy to see. Begin by making sure that your lory is not afraid of the target. A brazen little lory is likely to march right up and investigate right away, but it is always best to make sure you start off on the right foot with any training session—startling or scaring your lory is not the right foot.

When you present your target, say whatever your cue will be—something like "touch" works well—and wait for your lory to touch his beak or tongue to the colored tip of the target. When he does, say "good" and give him a treat. Repeat this until you again see that your lory understands what you want. Then, begin to move the target further away, so your lory has to walk a bit to get to the target, touch it, and get a treat. Once he has this behavior down, you can lead him anywhere with the target, even back into his cage if that's where you need him to go. This can be very handy if it is not a good time to handle him or if the person who needs to get him in the cage does not know him well.

Things to Remember

No matter what you are training, the time you spend with your lory should be fun. Keep your sessions short and be patient. If training becomes

Ending on a Positive Note

Always try to end your training session on a positive. If your bird is getting what you are teaching him, it is much better to end on that note than on a failure. Give him a big reward and stop. Both of you should be looking forward to the next training session. If you wait until he has lost interest and started to get frustrated, you may end up back where you started and with a bird who is not excited about training.

frustrating, it will not be fun for you or your lory, and neither of you will be likely to keep up the good work. Remember that training is fun time, and you will be amazed at the great things your bird can learn to do.

Behavior Problems

Most people who share their homes with parrots eventually have a behavior problem to solve. It is not that their birds are bad; it is just that it is very easy to accidentally encourage parrots to bite or scream. In fact, there are no bad birds–only bad behaviors that get reinforced. Generally speaking, these behaviors fall into the categories of biting, screaming, or plucking.

Biting

Biting is a last resort of parrots in the wild. When parrots become aggressive with one another in their natural habitat, they display body language in a variety of ways that warn a bite may be coming next. They may change the way they hold their feathers, head, or wings. A lory may arch his neck and hop in the direction of the bird he wants to drive out of his territory. In the wild, the bird on the receiving end of this posture will likely fly away before physical violence occurs. In our homes though, we rarely react appropriately to our parrot's body language.

A lory who displays body language that warns that we are in his space or that he does not like what we are doing expects that we understand what he is trying to tell us. If we do not listen, he may try other body language. When ultimately none of his body language works, he will resort to biting. Unfortunately, it is the biting that is likely to get us to move away or stop scratching him. The lory then learns that there is no reason to bother with all that other body language: his human won't listen to it anyway. So, he may begin to skip the subtleties and go straight for the bite. Learning to understand and react to your bird's body language is the first step in keeping the biting in your home to a minimum.

If you learn your lory's body language, you will also be able to recognize when your bird is so excited that he may nip

Your parrot may resort to biting to get what he wants, so it's critical to not reinforce this behavior.

at you. Biting can be self-reinforcing, meaning that just biting may get the bird what he wants. So, it is best to do everything you can to avoid getting bit, otherwise you have a long road ahead of you, reprogramming your bird that biting does not get him what he wants. When your lory is in an area where he is especially territorial, it may be best to target him to where you want him to go or ask that he step up on a perch instead of your hand. If he is out playing and gets wound up, it is best to end playtime until he calms down. Biting leads to more biting, so don't let it become a habit. Being bit does not have to be part of having a parrot.

Screaming

Some species of lory can be quite loud, but screaming is not a natural behavior. Screaming is a loud, repetitive, ongoing sound that a parrot does to get something he wants. Screaming is a learned behavior, not a natural one. And it is one of the easiest behaviors to accidently teach your parrot.

A screaming parrot is very difficult to ignore, so often when our bird starts screaming, we walk over and talk to him or play with him to distract him or because he just reminded us that he was in the room. The problem is that he quickly learns screaming will get him the attention that he wants. A parrot may scream because it gets you off the phone, gets you to leave the room, gets his cage covered at night when he's ready to go to bed, and for many other reasons. The trick to

Unfortunately, many pet parrots learn that screaming gets them attention. Teach your lory that being quiet earns him a reward.

retraining a parrot not to scream is to figure what it is that he is getting from all that screaming in the first place.

There is always a reason for a behavior that repeats itself, and if you can figure out why your parrot is screaming, you can either change what triggers the screaming or change what he gets for screaming. If you know what your parrot is hoping to get from his noise making, you can also teach him that a quieter sound gets your attention by only responding to him when he makes the more appropriate noise. Once a bird has learned that making a tremendous ruckus is the

Rewards for Training

Watch which fruits and veggies your lory chooses to eat first when you give him a bowl of goodies and use those for training. However, if you parrot does not seem to respond to food as a reward, treats are not the only way to reward a bird. With some birds, just being excited and getting praised can work. Other parrots will pay attention and work with you for their favorite toys. Figure out what works best for your lory.

best way to achieve something, it takes a long time to retrain a new behavior and to fade out the old one, but it can be done with patience and consistency. Of course, the best thing to do is to avoid accidentally encouraging the behavior in the first place. If you have a lory that is well-behaved, be mindful of paying attention to him when he is playing quietly and always take a moment to ask yourself what you are rewarding before you give him a treat or interact with him.

Plucking

Of all the behaviors that parrot owners struggle with, the most frustrating and difficult to manage is plucking. Plucking is different from preening and involves pulling out or snipping off feathers rather than letting them molt naturally. All parrot species seem to be capable of resorting to this behavior, but the reasons and level of plucking vary. Some parrots overpreen their primary wing feathers, some may just pluck the feathers around their legs and others may pluck every feather they can reach until they are bare. The reasons for plucking include illness, stress, nutrient deficiency, boredom, and habit. The challenge is to figure out why your lory is plucking.

If you notice your bird is beginning to pluck bare spots on his body, the first thing you should do is get him to the veterinarian. Your vet can test to make sure your bird is not suffering from zinc toxicity or some other illness. If your lory is given a clean bill of health, trying to decipher the reason for plucking can be challenging.

If there is anything that changed in your lory's environment right before he started plucking, immediately change it back to see if this might be the cause. Humans are not always good at guessing what might stress out a parrot, so start with a process of elimination. If you are fairly certain the plucking is not the result of a recent environmental change, the next step is to eliminate boredom.

Make sure that your busy-minded lory has plenty of environmental enrichment. Switch out old toys for new ones frequently. Teach him new tricks to keep his mind occupied. New and interesting things can keep him busy playing and investigating instead of plucking.

When you have tried everything and your lory is still plucking, don't despair. It can become a habit, like a person who bites her nails to the quick but is unable to stop. Keep encouraging new habits, but don't be too hard on yourself. Perhaps sometime in the future veterinarians will be able to come up with a definitive way to end plucking in parrots and other birds. In the mean time, there are many plucked parrots that live fine lives.

Getting Help

Training parrots and problem-solving bad behaviors can be very challenging. Being a good bird trainer takes practice and experience. Parrots are very different from the domestic pets with which most of us are used to sharing our homes. So, if you find yourself stumped, there is no shame in seeking help. And it is better to get help as soon as you find yourself facing a challenge than to wait until it is so bad you need to give up your lory.

If you know who bred your lory, your breeder is a good place to start for help. Remember that many people on the Internet claim to be experts and are happy to give you bad advice or sell you products promising to solve your problems overnight. Chances are the only thing they are going to do is take your money and make your problems worse. Someone who breeds lories will likely have suggestions on who can help you with your lory challenges. A parrot expert or a parrot behaviorist who uses solely positive reinforcement and understands applied behavioral analysis will be able to help you figure out why your parrot is biting or screaming and then develop a plan for retraining. Ask your veterinarian, local bird club, or parrot breeder for recommendations of who to hire.

Understanding a little bit about your parrot's behavior and taking the time to learn to train some simple behaviors can really make living with a lory enjoyable. And really, having fun with your parrot is the most important thing you can do. Lories are an absolute joy to have around, so take the time to enjoy your friendship!

The causes of feather plucking vary, so if your lory engages in this distressing behavior seek help from your veterinarian.

7

The Wide World of Lories

There are an amazing number of lory species, although not all of them are readily available in aviculture. Lories are, as a whole, the most beautifully feathered of all parrots, coming in a wide variety of colors and a range of sizes. All of these species of birds have the habits and build of a lory, but their personalities can be very different.

As you consider which of the lory species would make the right pet for you, be sure to do your homework. Since lories are no longer imported into the United States, the availability of species is limited to those already being bred in North America. Rarer species may be better left in a breeding situation, rather than kept as a single pet. Some lories may be too loud to keep in an apartment, and some tend to have a gentler personality than others. Rather than choosing your lory entirely on the beauty of the bird, make sure that he is an all-around right fit to be a pet in your home.

Black Lory

The black lory (*Chalcopsitta atra*) is a large lory from New Guinea and is striking in that he is almost entirely black. The tail is accented with red and yellow feathers underneath, but the rest of this lory's feathering is black with a purple sheen in the sunlight. There are very few parrots with black plumage, so although the black lory is not a brightly colored parrot, his coloration is unique and quite beautiful on close inspection. The black lory is 13 inches (32.5 cm) long with a rounded tail. Like all the *Chalcopsitta* lories, he has a shallow wing beat, which gives the appearance of his having a much slower and more labored flight than other lories.

Most of what is known about the black lory comes from aviculture. They are found mainly feeding in coconut palms and flowering trees along open areas like the coast, savannah, and lowland forest edge, but they have not

Duyvenbode's lory is closely related to the black lory. It originally hails from northern New Guinea.

been studied extensively. They are likely doing well in the wild. In captivity, they can be found in some breeding projects. Overall, they are thought to be one of the best pet species of lory. They can be noisy, but tame black lories enjoy interacting with people and tend to have gentle personalities.

Of the same genus, Duyvenbode's or brown lory (*C. duivenbodei*) is a very similar bird and also considered a wonderful pet. This lory is primarily brown with yellow accents. Duyvenbode's are available in American aviculture and are considered by lory enthusiasts to be a good choice as pets.

Blue-Streaked Lory

The blue-streaked lory (*Eos reticulata*) is a large, primarily red lory who is found in the Tanimbar Islands of Indonesia. They inhabit most habitats on the islands, including forest and agricultural land. They are about 12 inches (31 cm) long, and the most distinctive markings on them are a blue streak across the eyes that feathers into a narrow streak along the nape and mantle. This blue streaking is luminous in the sunlight and very striking.

Blue-streaked lories are beautiful

Blue-streaked lories have a very small range in the wild, and their population is decreasing.

parrots who are common in aviculture in the United States, as they are fairly easy to breed. They are sought-after pets. They can be loud and are very high-energy birds; however, they are gregarious, and hand-raised birds make enjoyable pets. Some blue-streaked lories also learn to talk. During the 1970s, they were regularly imported into Europe and the United States, but are no longer abundant in European

Endangered Lories

Here is a list of some lories who are currently endangered in their wild habitat:

- Red-throated Lorikeet (*Charmosyna amabilis*)   Critically Endangered
- New Caledonian Lorikeet (*Charmosyna diadema*)   Critically Endangered
- Blue-fronted Lorikeet (*Charmosyna toxopei*)   Critically Endangered
- Red-and-Blue Lory (*Eos histrio*)   Endangered
- Chattering Lory, Yellow-backed Lory (*Lorius garrulous*)   Endangered
- Rimitara Lorikeet, Kuhl's Lorikeet (*Vini kuhlii*)   Endangered
- Ultramarine Lorikeet (*Vini ultramarine*)   Endangered

From IUCN 2009. IUCN Red List of Threatened Species. Version 2009.1. <www.iucnredlist.org>. Downloaded on 20 July 2009.

aviculture. They are declining in their native habitat.

Red Lory

The red lory (*Eos bornea*) is an extremely common lory in U.S. aviculture and one of the most popularly kept species. It looks very similar to the blue-streaked lory, being almost entirely bright red with areas of black and blue on the wings. They are native to the Moluccan Islands, and two subspecies are found in U.S. aviculture, the Moluccan red lory and the Buru red lory. Habitat frequented by the red lory includes primarily wooded country, especially mangrove forests. They are rarely found in open areas.

The red lory is as well known for its beautiful plumage as for its loud voice, which it uses constantly. Their voice might make them unsuitable for apartment living and should also be a consideration for outdoor aviaries. Neighbors who are sensitive to noise may have issues with an aviary full of red lories. However, certain individuals have become excellent talkers, and

The red lory is one of the most popular pet species. Unfortunately, they tend to be very loud birds.

they are certainly beautiful as well as readily available.

Dusky Lory

The dusky lory (*Pseudeos fuscata*) has two color phases–yellow and orange–and even within these phases the shade of coloration can vary. They have perhaps the most varied plumage of all the lories species. They are found in New Guinea in almost all habitats from sea level up to 5,000 feet (1,524 m). They tend to travel in noisy flocks, flying long distances between their roosting and feeding grounds. They are about 10 inches (25 cm) long, which makes them a manageably sized bird for many handlers. They are easily bred in captivity and readily available.

Dusky lories are one of the more popular species available in the United States, and for those who really love the "lory" personality, they are very enjoyable companions. Lory enthusiasts describe them as being "extreme lories," with all the typical characteristics of a lory, amplified. They are energetic, willful, very gregarious, and vocal. Sometimes dusky lories can be aggressive, so they may not be the right bird for someone who is new to parrots and may be intimidated. For some parrot owners, their high-pitched loud voice might be too much. However, for those who don't mind their noise, the trade off is that some individuals can learn to talk.

Rainbow Lorikeet

The most popular and perhaps

Dusky lories are best for experienced parrot owners. They can be very willful birds, but do make good pets for the right person.

most well-know of all the lories is the rainbow lorikeet (*Trichoglossus haematodus*). These are among the most beautiful lories, feathered in a gorgeous array of bright colors and with a big personality to match. There are over 20 different subspecies of this species of lory, and about eight of these have been available at one time or another in American aviculture. Although each subspecies looks very similar, their coloration can be different. They are native to different areas of Australia and the South Pacific.

The rainbow lorikeet is about 12 inches (30 cm) long. Their size can

There are numerous subspecies of the rainbow lorikeet, and several of these are present in aviculture. Shown here are (clockwise from top left) the green-naped lorikeet, Edward's lorikeet, the red-collared lorikeet (*T. h. rubritorquis*), and Swainson's lorikeet. The red-collared and Edward's lorikeets are often considered species separate from the rainbow lorikeet.

vary by a couple of inches depending on the subspecies. They have an electric blue head, with an orange breast, a yellow-green collar, and a green back. They have a bright orange beak and a long pointed tail.

They are an incredibly common bird in the wild and are spread across a variety of habitats including mallee scrub, open eucalyptus forest, rainforest, and even gardens and parks.

As long as there is sufficient food, the rainbow lory is likely to appear in its native habitat. They are also likely to appear in large flocks when artificial food sites are created.

Lory enthusiasts believe that the personalities of the various subspecies of lories can be very different and that some are more suitable as pets than others. So, it is a good idea to investigate the various subspecies and decide which one is right for you before you bring a lorikeet into your home.

Green-Naped Lorikeet
The green-naped lorikeet (*T. h. haematodus*) is considered the nominate subspecies and is the most common of the subspecies available in American aviculture. These birds are native to New Guinea and Indonesia. They have a red breast with feather edges lined in blue. They also have a greenish yellow collar. The green-naped has a reputation for being nippy.

Edward's Lorikeet
The Edward's lorikeet (*T. h. capistratus*) has a yellow upper breast with feathers tipped in red. The neck band is yellow. They have a primarily green body with a blue forehead, crown, and chin. They are native to Timor and are relatively shy compared to other subspecies. Their more relaxed nature, when compared to the more boisterous and quarrelsome nature of other rainbow lories, makes some lory experts feel this subspecies is most suitable as pets.

Swainson's or Blue Mountain Lorikeet
The Swainson's lorikeet (*T. h. moluccanus*) is native to eastern Australia. They tend to be nomadic but set up residence in areas of human habitation where food is plentiful. They are probably the most well-known of all the rainbow lorikeets and have been found in aviculture since 1771. They have a dark blue head and abdomen, with an orange breast. They do not have the blue-tipped breast feathers of green-naped lorikeets. They also have a yellow-green collar.

Goldie's Lorikeet
The Goldie's lorikeet (*Psitteuteles goldiei* or *Trichoglossus goldiei*) is native to a wide range of the mountains of New Guinea, where they are fairly abundant. They travel in groups of 30 individuals or more, making long daily flights from roosting sites to feeding areas in the midstorey and canopy of flowering trees. This species is also common in American aviculture, although it is less common in England and Australia.

Goldie's lorikeet is often recommended as a good choice for those who have not had a lory before. This species is a little mellower than others.

Lories Species Most Likely to Talk

Keep in mind that just because a species is likely to talk does not mean that an individual bird will. However, if you are hoping that your lory might talk, these species are known for mimicking human words:

- Black-capped lory
- Blue-streaked lory
- Chattering lory
- Red lory

They are small, only 7 inches (19 cm) long, with a scarlet crown and forehead and a mauve stripe across the eyes. They have a black beak and brown irises. They are primarily a green bird, with the streaking of light and dark shades on their chest resembling the markings on a watermelon.

There is some discussion whether the Goldie's lorikeet belongs to the genus *Psitteuteles* or *Trichoglossus*. Either way, this is a fantastic little lory, and many lory enthusiasts feel that Goldie's lorikeets are excellent first lories. If they do talk, it is in tiny, squeaky, difficult-to-understand words, and their voices overall are not as loud as many species. They are small but full of personality. Goldie's lorikeets do not seem to have the aggressive tendencies that characterize many other lory species. However, they still have the brazen lory personality, and their small size can get them into endless trouble if not closely monitored.

In nature, chattering lories are found in pairs instead of flocks. This species tends to be aggressive to other parrots.

Chattering Lory

The chattering lory (*Lorius garrulous*) is a large, stocky bird; it is 12 inches (30 cm) long and is primarily scarlet. They occasionally have a few yellow feathers within the red, and their wings and thighs are green. Their beaks and irises are orange, and the skin around the eye and on the cere is gray. They are native to the northern Moluccan Islands in Indonesia. Although a large wild population still exists, it is on the decline due to habitat loss and capture for the pet trade. Fortunately, it is believed that trapping for the pet trade has greatly diminished.

The chattering lory is a common bird in American and English aviculture and is a sought-after pet because of his personality. They are extremely active, outgoing, and have a tendency to be excellent talkers. They are very interactive when tame, and many lory enthusiasts consider them to be a good first lory. However, they can be aggressive toward other parrot-like species. They can be loud, but do not tend to use their loudest normal vocalizations often. There are two subspecies, the nominate race and the yellow-backed (*L. g. flavopallaitus*), which has a splash of yellow on its back.

Black-Capped Lory

The black-capped lory (*Lorius lory*) is found in New Guinea and adjacent smaller islands. They are primarily birds of the lowland forests and are

Black-capped lories are very loud, and it usually is best to keep them in outdoor aviaries.

uncommon above 3,280 feet (1,000 m). The black-capped lory is fairly common in aviculture. They are brightly colored birds who are prone to mimicry. Be warned that they have loud voices and may not be desirable for keeping indoors. These are colorful and relatively large lories at about 12 inches long (30 cm) with a stocky body and a broad long tail.

There are at least six recognized subspecies; all have a black forehead, nape, and crown, while the rest of the head is red. The body around the wings also is red. Their wings are green on top and gray-yellow underneath. The legs and belly are blue. There is no coloration difference between males and females; however, juvenile birds have a larger patch of dark blue on their breast than adults. Juveniles also have a brown beak that gradually turns dark yellow as they mature. Most of the subspecies of black-capped lory remain common in the wild, but the subspecies *L. l. cyanuchen* is relatively rare, with fewer than 5,000 individuals remaining.

Blue-Crowned Lorikeet

The blue-crowned lorikeet (*Vini australis*) is a smaller lory measuring about 7.5 inches (19 cm) long. They are primarily green birds with red and blue markings on the face and belly. They have orange beaks and feet. This species has gone extinct on a few of the islands that were once in his natural range, although he is fairly common in other parts of the range. The biggest challenge these little parrots face is the introduction of rats, which raid their nests and eat their eggs. They are found in Fiji, Samoa, Tonga, and on Niue, one of the Cook Islands.

This is a fairly rare species in aviculture, but has been successfully bred in North America and may become more readily available to zoos and private aviculture in the future. The San Diego Zoo, which has an amazing lory collection, currently breeds blue-crowned lorikeets. The genus *Vini* has some of the least known lory species in aviculture, and most of the species are struggling in the wild. With the end of importation, it is important that any of the *Vini* lories in aviculture be put into breeding situations so that the captive population can grow.

Musk lorikeets are rare in American aviculture but are common aviary birds in their native Australia.

Musk Lorikeet

The musk lorikeet (*Glossopsitta concinna*) is a medium-sized, primarily green lorikeet. They are about 9 inches (22 cm) long. They have some yellow in a patch on the side of the breast that is mostly covered by the wings. They also have a red forehead and red ear coverts with a crown of blue and a bronze mantle. The musk lorikeet is a nomadic species found in eastern and southeastern Australia and Tasmania. They are found in most available habitats in their range from coastal scrubs to open forest, congregating anywhere that flowering or fruiting trees are found. It is not unusual to see them mixed in with a flock with other species of Australian lorikeets. They are doing well in the wild.

They are active lories and are reported to be wonderful birds in a mixed aviary because they do not have a tendency to be aggressive toward other birds. They are very common aviary birds in their native Australia, but strict exportation laws have kept them from being common elsewhere. They are found occasionally in American aviculture and are a quieter bird than the rainbow lorikeet, with a more subdued personality. They may be able to learn to talk but are more adept at

Stella's lorikeet is found in two color varieties, the normal and the melanistic (the dark-colored bird in this photo).

imitating noises, such as the microwave and telephone. Since they are not very abundant in American aviculture, it is probably best to place them in a breeding situation than to keep them as pets until they become more numerous.

Papaun Lorikeet

The Papaun lorikeet (*Charmosyna papou*) is gorgeous and unmistakable. It is the only species with a long trailing tail. The length of the body is about 7 inches (17 cm), but with the tail their length is 16 inches (17 cm). Their main plumage is red, but they have dark green wings and mantle. A black patch streaked with blue runs across their eyes. They are also accented with yellow and black. The females have less yellow on their flanks than males. The most common subspecies found in American aviculture is the Stella's lorikeet (*C. p. stellae*), which is found in a normal color phase, as well as in a melanistic or dark colored phase. In the wild, they range through the mountains of southeastern New Guinea and their population is doing well.

Stella's lorikeet is considered by enthusiasts to be a wonderful bird with a great personality. They are very playful and energetic. Stella's lorikeets are also very quiet in comparison to other species and become very tame and interactive with humans. However, they can be aggressive with other parrot-like birds, so they may not be a good bird to have in a mixed aviary or mixed-parrot household. They are also a rather high-priced species.

Yellow-Billed or Musschenbroek's Lorikeet

The Musschenbroek's lorikeet

(*Neopsittacus musschenbroekii*) is a medium-sized lory, about 9 inches (23 cm) long. It is a primarily green bird with plumage that becomes more yellowish toward the underparts. It has an olive-brown nape, and the crown is green and streaked with yellow. The throat, breast, and abdomen are red. In the wild, it is found in the mountains of New Guinea, mainly residing in the montane forest, forest edges, and partially cleared areas at 5,000 to 8,500 ft (1,524 to 2,591 m). They are fast flyers and excellent climbers. The Musschenbroek's lorikeet has been frequently observed to run "rodent-like" along branches, keeping its head down as it scurries. Their diet is more varied than most lory species, and their beak is more similar to a seed-eating parrot than that of many other lories.

The Musschenbroek's lorikeets are occasionally found in American aviculture, but most frequently in aviary situations. They do well in

Queen's Lory

The Rimatara lorikeet (*Vini kuhlii*) in French Polynesia has a wonderful conservation story. About 100 years ago, the Queen of Rimatara forbade any harm be done to the remaining small population of Rimatara lorikeets, a gorgeous red, yellow, green, and blue lory that was frequently hunted for its feathers. Between humans and invasive rat species, the lory was struggling to survive, and the Queen's protection helped them. Then, in 2007, another Queen, the Queen of Atiu in the Cook Islands gave the Rimatara lorikeet another hand. She accompanied 27 of the birds back to her island, which had excellent habitat but where the lories had long ago disappeared. Since its reintroduction to Atiu, the Rimatara lorikeet has continued to do well and is even breeding on their new island home.

Musschenbroek's lorikeet—or muschies as they are known affectionately—do very well in aviaries but usually do not make good household pets.

mixed aviaries and seem to not be as aggressive toward other parrot-like birds as many of the lory species. Generally though, their personality makes them unsuitable as pets.

Closing thoughts

These are only a few of the species of lories available in aviculture, including several of those most commonly available. If a particular species seems like the right fit for your home and personality, do some further research. If possible, visit a zoo or aviary that features the bird of your dreams. If the species you've set your heart on is not readily available where you live, don't give up. With further searching and research, you may discover that a similar and more readily available species may be for sale in your area. When considering lory ownership, it's important to take your time when choosing your ideal bird. You will likely be looking at a 20-year commitment, so you'll want to find a perfect match.

Lories have captivated bird lovers for thousands of years in the wild and for centuries in aviculture, although they've had a bad reputation for a long time as messy and difficult to maintain. Their diet *is* challenging, but some good commercial nectars are on the market now, and, in many ways, lories are no more difficult to clean up after than any other parrot. They just make a different kind of mess. Aviculturists and scientists have learned a great deal about them in recent decades, and this has led to lories becoming an increasingly popular pet. If you find yourself captivated by a lory species and do not mind the challenges, you may find they are the perfect fit for your household. So, enjoy your lory. He is sure to bring color and personality to your home!

Resources

Organizations

American Federation of Aviculture
P.O.Box 7312
N. Kansas City, MO 64116
Telephone: (816) 421-3214
Fax: (816)421-3214
E-mail: afaoffice@aol.com
www.afabirds.org

American Lory Society
PO Box 334
Escondido, CA 92033
www.lorysociety.com/

Avicultural Society of America
PO Box 5516
Riverside, CA 92517-5516
Telephone: (951) 780-4102
Fax: (951) 789-9366
E-mail: info@asabirds.org
www.asabirds.org

Aviculture Society of the United
Kingdom
Arcadia-The Mounts-East Allington-
Totnes
Devon TQ9 7QJ
United Kingdom
E-mail: admin@avisoc.co.uk
www.avisoc.co.uk/

International Association of Avian
Trainers and Educators
350 St. Andrews Fairway
Memphis, TN 38111
Telephone: (901) 685-9122
Fax: (901) 685-7233
E-mail: secretary@iaate.org
www.iaate.org

International Lory Society
10101A Tucker Jones Rd.
Riverview, FL 33569

The Parrot Society of Australia
P.O. Box 75
Salisbury, Queensland 4107
Australia
E-mail: petbird@parrotsociety.org.au
www.partosociety.org.au

Emergency Resources and Rescue Organizations

ASPCA Animal Poison Control Center
Telephone: (888) 426-4435
E-mail: napcc@aspca.org (for non-
emergency, general information only)
www.apcc.aspca.org

Bird Hotline
P.O. Box 1411
Sedona, AZ 86339-1411
E-mail: birdhotline@birdhotline.com
www.birdhotline.com/

Bird Placement Program
P.O. Box 347392
Parma, OH 44134
Telephone: (330) 722-1627
E-mail: birdrescue5@hotmail.com
www.birdrescue.com

The Gabriel Foundation
1025 Acoma Street
Denver, CO 80204
Telephone: (970) 963-2620
Fax: (970) 963-2218
E-mail: gabriel@thegabrielfoundation.org
www.thegabrielfoundation.org

Parrot Rehabilitation Society
P.O. Box 620213
San Diego, CA 92102
Telephone: (619) 224-6712
E-mail: prsorg@yahoo.com
www.parrotsociety.org

Petfinder
www.petfinder.com

Veterinary Resources
Association of Avian Veterinarians
P.O.Box 811720
Boca Raton, FL 33481-1720
Telephone: (561) 393-8901
Fax: (561) 393-8902
E-mail: AAVCTRLOFC@aol.com
www.aav.org

Exotic Pet Vet.Net
www.exoticpetvet.net

Internet Resources
AvianWeb
www.avianweb.com/

BirdCLICK
www.geocities.com/Heartland/
Acres/9154/

HolisticBird.org
www.holisticbird.org

Loriinae Exotics
www.loriinae.com/

Lorikeets.com
www.lorikeets.com/

LoryMagic.com
www.lorymagic.com/

The Parrot Pages
www.parrotpages.com

Parrot Parrot
www.parrotparrot.com/

Pet Bird Lory FAQ
www.upatsix.com/faq/loryfaq.html

Conservation Organizations
Kakapo Recovery Programme
www.kakaporecovery.org.nz

Loro Parque Foundation
Avenida Loro Parque s/n - 38400
Puerto de la Cruz
Tenerife, Canary Islands
Spain
Telephone.: +34 922 37 38 41
Fax: +34 922 37 50 21
www.loroparque-fundacion.org

Macaw Landing Foundation
P.O. Box 17364
Portland, OR 97217
www.macawlanding.org/index.shtml

ProAves
www.proaves.org/sommaire.

php?lang=en
Rare Species Conservatory Foundation
www.rarespecies.org/

World Parrot Trust (UK)
Glarmor House
Hayle, Cornwall TR27 4HB
Telephone: 444 01736 751 026
Fax: 44 01736 751 028
E-mail: uk@worldparrottrust.org
www.worldparrottrust.org

World Parrot Trust (USA)
P.O.Box 353
Stillwater, MN 55082
Telephone: (651) 275-1877
Fax: (651)275-1891
E-mail: usa@worldparrottrus.org
www.worldparrottrust.org

Magazines

Bird Talk
3 Burroughs
Irvine, CA 92618
Telephone: 949-855-8822
Fax: (949) 855-3045
www.birdtalkmagazine.com

Good Bird
PO Box 150604
Austin, TX 78715
E-mail: Info@goodbirdinc.com
www.GoodBirdInc.com

Parrots Magazine
The Old Cart House
Applesham Farm
Coombes, West Sussex
BN15 0RP
United Kingdom
Telephone: +44 (0) 1273 464 777
Fax: +44 (0) 1273 463 999
E-mail: info@imaxweb.co.uk
www.parrotmag.com

Books

Deutsch, Robin. *The Click That Does the Trick*. TFH Publications, Inc.

Deutsch, Robin. *The Healthy Bird Cookbook*. TFH Publications, Inc.

Heidenreich, Barbara. *The Parrot Problem Solver.*TFH Publications, Inc.

Moutsaki, Nikki. *Your Outta Control Bird*. TFH Publications, Inc.

O'Connor, Rebecca K. *A Parrot for Life*. TFH Publications, Inc.

Rach, Julie. *The Simple Guide to Bird Care and Training*. TFH Publications, Inc.

Index

Boldfaced numbers indicate illustrations.

A
ABVP (American Board of Veterinary Practitioners), 64
accessories, living area, 30–32
acclimating, 51–53
acrobatics, **6**, 10
airborne irritants, 34
Allium schoenoprasum (chives), 44
Amazon parrot, **67**
American Board of Veterinary Practitioners (ABVP), 64
Anthemis nobilis (chamomile flowers), 44
antibiotics, 73
aspergillosis (infection), 72
Aspergillus (fungus), 72
Association of Avian Veterinarians, 64
Atiu, Queen of, 104
attention span, 79
aviaries, 6, **7**. *See also* cages
avocados, 46

B
bacterial infections, 67, 70–71
banding, 9
bath pans, 31, 56
bathing, 55–56, **55**
beak
    care of, 56–58, **57**
    characteristics of, 10, 28
behavior
    body language and, 79–80, **81, 82**
    natural environment and, 78–79, **78**
    temperament and, 10–12, **11**
behavior problems
    biting, 88–89, **88**
    plucking, 90–91, **91**
    screaming, 89–90, **89**
Bellis perennis (daisies), 44
bird sitters, 59–60, **59**
bird trainers, 91
bites, 67
black lory (*Chalcopsitta atra*), 15, 94–95
black-capped lory (*Lorius lory*), 100, 101–102, **101**
blood feather, broken, 66–67, **67**
blue mountain lorikeet (*Trichoglossus h. moluccanus*), **98**, 99
blue-crowned lorikeet (*Vini australis*), 102
blue-fronted lorikeet (*Charmosyna toxopei*), 96
blue-streaked lory (*Eos reticulata*), **7**, **15**, 95–96, **95**, 100
boarding your lory, 59–60
body language, 79–80, **81, 82**
bottlebrush (*Callistemon* spp.), **38,** 44
bowls, feeding, 31
broad-tailed lory, 16
brown lory (*Chalcopsitta duivenbodei)*, **94**, 95

C
cages
    cleaning, 28–30
    hospital cages, 66
    indoor, 22–24
    outdoor, 25–26
    pest controls for, 30
    placement of, 23
    safety considerations, 33–34
    size, 23
    sleeping, 26–27

Calendula officinalis (calendula), 44
Callistemon spp. (bottlebrush), **38,** 44
Candida (fungus), 72–73
candidiasis (thrush), 72
cardinal lory (*Chalcopsitta cardinals*), **13**
carnation (*Dianthus caryophyllus*), 44
Chalcopsitta
    general characteristics, 14–15
    atra, 15, 94–95
    cardinals, **13**
    duivenbodei, **94**, 95
chamomile flowers (*Anthemis nobilis* and *Matricaria recutita*), 44
Charmosyna
    general characteristics, 15
    amabilis, 96
    diadema, 96
    p. stellae, 15, **103**, 104
    papou, 103–104
    toxopei, 96
chattering lory (*Lorius garrulus garrulus*), 16, 96, 100, **100**, 101
children and lories, 14
chives (*Allium schoenoprasum*), 44
Chlamydiaphila psittaci (bacteria), 71
choosing a lory, 13–14
cleaning cages, 28–30, **29**
clicker training, 86
coccidiosis (parasite), 74
collared lory, **17**, 18
consistency in training, 81–82

D
daisies (*Bellis perennis*), 44
dangerous foods, 46–47
Dianthus caryophyllus (carnation), 44
diet. *See* food
dietary problems, 70, **71**
DNA sexing, 7, 68–69
dusky lory (*Pseudeos fuscata*), 18, **24**, **55**, 97, **97**
Duyvenbode's lory (*Chalcopsitta duivenbodei*), **94**, 95

E
E. coli, 71
edible flowers, 44
edible toys, 33
Edward's lorikeet (*Trichoglossus h. capistratus*), **98**, 99
egg binding, 69–70
egg laying, 70
elderberry flowers (*Sambucus canadensis*), 44
emergency care, 66–70
endangered lories, 96
environment, changes in
    acclimating, 51–53
    quarantine, 50–51, **50**
environmental enrichment, 32–33
Eos
    general characteristics, 15–16
    bornea, 96–97, **96**, 100
    histrio, 96
    reticulata, **7**, **15**, 16, 95–96, **95**, 100
eucalyptus flowers (*Eucalyptus* spp.), 44
event markers in training, 84

F
feathers
    care of, 55–56
    losing, 72
feet
    characteristics of, 10
    toys for, 32–33
female vs. male, 12
finding a lory to adopt, 12–13
first-aid kits, 68

flying outside of cage, 34–35
food
    avocados, 46
    dangerous foods, 46–47
    diet, new thoughts on, 43–44
    diet, old thoughts on, 40
    edible flowers, 44
    foraging for, 33
    frequency of feeding, 44–45
    freshness of, 34, 40
    fruits, 41–42, **43**
    grapes, 51–52, **51**
    homemade, 40
    live food, 45
    nectar, 40–41, **41**
    nutrition in, 38–40
    pellets, 43, **47**
    placement of, **35**
    spouts, 42
    sugar, 42, 44
    supplements, 39
    time-saving tips, 47
    vegetables, 41–42, **45**
    water requirements, 45–46
foraging for food, 33
fractures, 68
fringe parrots, 18
fruit flies, 60
fruits, 41–42, **43**
fungal infections, 71–73

G
galvanized wire cages, 24
gladiolus (*Gladiolus* spp.), 44
Glossopsitta
    general characteristics, 16
    concinna, 16, **65**, 102–103, **102**
    porphyrocephala, 16
glossy lory, 14
Goldie's lorikeet (*Psitteuteles goldiei* or *Trichoglossus goldiei*), **27**, 99–100, **99**
grapes, 51–52, **51**
green-napped lorikeet (*Trichoglossus h. haematodus*), **98**, 99
grit, 46
grooming, 53–54
grooming health checks, 56
grooming supplies, 56

H
hand-raised lories, 14, 18
hanging toys, 32–33
health checks, 56
health guarantees, 13
health issues
    bacterial infections, 70–71
    dietary problems, 70, **71**
    emergency care, 66–70
    fungal infections, 71–73
    parasites, 73–74
    psittacine beak and feather disease, 74–75
    signs of ill health, 65–66, **65**
    veterinarians, locating, 64, **64**
    well-check-ups, 64–65
healthy characteristics, 13–14
hemochromatosis (iron storage disease), 70
hibiscus (*Hibiscus rosa-sinensis*), 44
hospital cages, 66
house plants, **69**
household, moving with your lory, 60–61
household pets, 35, 53
housing. *See* cages

I

impatiens (*Impatiens walleriana*), 44
indoor cages, 22–24
ineffective training techniques, 80
iron storage disease, 70

K
Kuhl's lorikeet (*Vini kuhlii*), 19, 96, 104

L
lead poisoning, 68–69
leg bands, 9
legs, characteristics of, 10
lice, 73–74
life span, 52
lighting, 31–32
lilac (*Syringa vulgaris*), 44
live food, 45
living area accessories, 30–32
loose lories, 53
Lorius
    general characteristics, 16
    chlorocercus, **16**
    g. flavopallaitus, 96, 101
    garrulus garrulus, 16, 96, 100, **100**, 101
    l. cyanuchen, 102
    lory, 100, 101–102, **101**
lory basics
    lory vs. lorikeet, 8
    overview, 6–8
    types of, 14–19
lost lories, 58

M
male vs. female, 12
marigold (*Tagetes patula*), 44
Matricaria recutita (chamomile flowers), 44
McDonald, Debra, 43, 44
milk thistle (*Silybum marianum*), 44
mites, 73–74
molting feathers, 72
moving household with your lory, 60–61
multi-pet households, 25, 34, 53, 61, **73**
Musk lorikeet (*Glossopsitta concinna*), 16, **65**, 102–103, **102**
Musschenbroek's lorikeet (*Neopsittacus musschenbroekii*), 17, 104–105, **105**
Mycobacterium (bacterial infection), 71

N
nail trimming, 56–58
nasturtiums (*Tropaeolum majus*), 44
native habitat feeding customs, 38–39
nectar, 40–41, **41**
Neopsittacus
    general characteristics, 17
    musschenbroekii, **16**, 17, 104–105, **105**
nestboxes, 28
New Caledonian lorikeet (*Charmosyna diadema*), 96
nutrition, 38–40. *See also* food

O
Oreopsittacus
    general characteristics, 17
    arfaki, 17
other pets and lories, 35, 53
outdoor cages, 25–26

P
pansies (*Viola X wittrockiana*), 44
Papaun lorikeet (*Charmosyna papou*), 103–104
parasites, 73–74
parrot fever, 71
passionflower (*Passiflora* spp.), 44
Pasteurella multocida (bacteria), 67

PBFD (Psittacine beak and feather disease), 74–75
pellet food, 43, **47**
perches, 30–31, **30**
pest controls for cages, 30
Phigys
    general characteristics, 17–18
    solitarus, **17**, 18
physical characteristics, 9–10. *See also specific species*
play areas, 27–28, **27**
plum-faced lorikeet (*Oreopsittacus arfaki*), 17
poisoning, 34, 68–69
positive reinforcement, 80–81, 87
preening, **54**, 55
professional help with training, 91
Pseudeos
    general characteristics, 18
    fuscata, 18, **24**, **55**, 97, **97**
psittacine beak and feather disease (PBFD), 74–75
Psitteuteles goldiei, **27**, 99–100, **99**
purple-crowned lorikeet, 16

Q
quarantine, 50–51, **50**, **73**
queen's lory, 104

R
rainbow lory (*Trichoglossus haematodus*), **7**, 18, **19**, 97–99, **98**
red lory (*Eos bornea*), 96–97, **96**, 100
red-and-blue lory (*Eos histrio*), 96
red-collared lorikeet (*Trichoglossus h. rubritorquis*), **98**
red-throated lorikeet (*Charmosyna amabilis*), 96
rewards, **83**, 90
Rimatara, Queen of, 104
Rimitara lorikeet (*Vini kuhlii*), 19, 96, 104
roses (*Rosa* spp.), 44
rotating toys, 33

S
safety considerations, 33–34
sage (*Salvia officinalis*), 44
Salmonella, 71
Sambucus canadensis (elderberry flowers), 44
San Diego Zoo, 102
scaly-breasted lory, **29**
Schmit, Matt, 45
signs of ill health, 65–66, **65**
Silybum marianum (milk thistle), 44
size
    of cages, 23
    of lories, 9
sleeping cages, 26–27
smoke hazards, 34
spouts, 42
stationing training, 86–87
Stella's lorikeet (*Charmosyna p. stellae*), 15, **103**, 104
step-up training, 84–86, **85**
stick training, 85–86
stress, 74
substrate, 29
sugar, 42, 44
sunflower seeds, 46
supplements, food, 39
suspended aviaries, 26
Swainson's lorikeet (*Trichoglossus h. moluccanus*), **98**, 99
swallowing hazards, 34
Syringa vulgaris (lilac), 44

T
Tagetes patula (marigold), 44
talking lories, 11, 100
taming, 82–84
targeting training, 87
Teflon, 34

temperament and behavior, 10–12, **11**
thrush, 72
tongue characteristics, **8**, 9
toys, **31**, 32–33, **32**
training
    attention span, 79
    body language and, 79–80, **81**, **82**
    clicker training, 86
    consistency in, 81–82
    event markers, 84
    ineffective techniques, 80
    positive reinforcement, 80–81, 87
    professional help with, 91
    rewards, **83**, 90
    stationing, 86–87
    step-up training, 84–86, **85**
    stick training, 85–86
    taming, 82–84
    targeting, 87
traveling with your lory, 58–59
Trichoglossus
    general characteristics, 18
    goldiei, **27**, 99–100, **99**
    h. capistratus, **98**, 99
    h. haematodus, **98**, 99
    h. moluccanus, **98**, 99
    h. rubritorquis, **98**
    haematodus, **7**, 18, **19**, 97–99, **98**
Tropaeolum majus (nasturtiums), 44

U
Ultramarine lorikeet (*Vini ultramarine*), 96
unweaned parrots, 18

V
vegetable flowers, 44
vegetables, 41–42, **45**
veterinarians, 64, **64**
Vini
    general characteristics, 18–19
    australis, 102
    kuhlii, 19, 96, 104
    ultramarine, 96
Viola X wittrockiana (pansies), 44
violet-necked lory, **6**
violets (*Viola odorata*), 44
virgin parrots, 18

W
walk-in aviaries, 25–26, **25**
water requirements, 45–46
well-check-ups, 64–65
whiskered lorikeet (*Oreopsittacus arfaki*), 17
Wilhemina's lorikeet, 9
wing clipping, 54–55
wounds, 67

Y
yeast (fungus), 72–73
yellow-backed lory (*Lorius garrulous flavopallaitus*), 96, 101
Yellow-billed lorikeet (*Neopsittacus musschenbroekii*), **16**, 17, 104–105, **105**
yellow-streaked lory, 9

Z
zinc poisoning, 34, 68–69

About the Author

Rebecca K. O'Connor has trained birds professionally in zoos and private facilities around the United States and abroad. She has been a falconer and parrot keeper for two decades and has experience working with a tremendous variety of animals. Having cared for and worked with several lory species, her favorite is Goldie's lorikeet. She shares her Northern California home with three parrots, two falcons, and a Brittany. She is the author of the best-selling *A Parrot for Life.*

Photo Credits

Larry Allan: 27, 67
Greg Atkinson: 29
John Austin (from Shutterstock): 8
Kitch Bain (from Shutterstock): 6
Joan Balzarini: 30, 31, 47, 51, 55, 75, 89, 99, 100
Craig Barhorst (from Shutterstock): 91
Paul-André Belle-Isle (from Shutterstock): 50
Blue Soul Photography (from Shutterstock): 85
Chubbster (from Shutterstock): 16
Philip Date (from Shutterstock): 65
Lindsey Eltinge (from Shutterstock): 1, 52, 76
Richard Fitzer (from Shutterstock): 69
Isabelle Francais: 45, 82, 83, 88
Insuratelu Gabriela Gianina (from Shutterstock): 94
Rui Manuel Teles Gomes (from Shutterstock): 35
gracious_tiger (from Shutterstock): 59
Daniel Herbert (from Shutterstock): 10, 64
Andrew Kua Seng How (from Shutterstock): 19
David Hsu (from Shutterstock): 95
Dee Hunter (from Shutterstock): 4, 36
Eric Ilasenko: 98 (upper right, lower right)
Imagemaker (from Shutterstock): 20

Eric Isselée (from Shutterstock): 13
J_S (from Shutterstock): 11
Viljar Kivi (from Shutterstock): 61
Khoo Si Lin (from Shutterstock): 73
Manamana (from Shutterstock): 96
Xavier Marchant (from Shutterstock): 43
Chad McDermott (from Shutterstock): 62
Alta Oosthuizen (from Shutterstock): 24
Mark William Penny (from Shutterstock): 81
Andrej Pol (from Shutterstock): 102
Aspen Rock (from Shutterstock): 101
Rovenko Design (from Shutterstock): 38
Jean-Edouard Rozey (from Shutterstock): 54
Dick Schroeder: 103, 105
Sim Kay Seng (from Shutterstock): 48, 57
Chai Kian Shin (from Shutterstock): 98 (upper left)
Jordan Tan (from Shutterstock): 78, 92
John C. Tyson: 32
John Williams (from Shutterstock): 97
Worldswildlifewonders (from Shutterstock): 17
Arnaud Zehnder (from Shutterstock): 71
Alesssandro Zocc (from Shutterstock): 15